Cambridge Elements

Elements in the History of Philosophy
and Theology in the West
edited by
Alexander J. B. Hampton
University of Toronto

LEO XIII AND THE RISE OF NEO-THOMISM

Valfredo Maria Rossi
Italian Ministry of Culture

Shaftesbury Road, Cambridge CB2 8EA, United Kingdom

One Liberty Plaza, 20th Floor, New York, NY 10006, USA

477 Williamstown Road, Port Melbourne, VIC 3207, Australia

314–321, 3rd Floor, Plot 3, Splendor Forum, Jasola District Centre, New Delhi – 110025, India

103 Penang Road, #05–06/07, Visioncrest Commercial, Singapore 238467

Cambridge University Press is part of Cambridge University Press & Assessment, a department of the University of Cambridge.

We share the University's mission to contribute to society through the pursuit of education, learning and research at the highest international levels of excellence.

www.cambridge.org
Information on this title: www.cambridge.org/9781009660532

DOI: 10.1017/9781009660563

© Valfredo Maria Rossi 2025

This publication is in copyright. Subject to statutory exception and to the provisions of relevant collective licensing agreements, no reproduction of any part may take place without the written permission of Cambridge University Press & Assessment.

When citing this work, please include a reference to the DOI 10.1017/9781009660563

First published 2025

A catalogue record for this publication is available from the British Library

ISBN 978-1-009-66053-2 Hardback
ISBN 978-1-009-66052-5 Paperback
ISSN 3033-3954 (online)
ISSN 3033-3946 (print)

Cambridge University Press & Assessment has no responsibility for the persistence or accuracy of URLs for external or third-party internet websites referred to in this publication and does not guarantee that any content on such websites is, or will remain, accurate or appropriate.

For EU product safety concerns, contact us at Calle de José Abascal, 56, 1°, 28003 Madrid, Spain, or email eugpsr@cambridge.org

Leo XIII and the Rise of Neo-Thomism

Elements in the History of Philosophy and Theology in the West

DOI: 10.1017/9781009660563
First published online: November 2025

Valfredo Maria Rossi
Italian Ministry of Culture
Author for correspondence: Valfredo Maria Rossi, valfremdm@gmail.com

Abstract: This Element examines the historical context and intellectual implications of the Thomistic revival inaugurated by Pope Leo XIII's encyclical *Aeterni Patris*, pursuing two principal objectives. First, this Element demonstrates that *Aeterni Patris* represented a decisive turning point in Catholic philosophical and theological thought: it not only revitalised Thomism but also brought an end to the doctrinal pluralism that had characterised nineteenth-century Catholicism. Second, the study argues that the Thomistic revival envisioned by Leo XIII was not a neutral academic enterprise concerned merely with a renewed engagement with Aquinas's doctrine, but rather an ideological initiative rooted in the framework of intransigent Catholicism, wherein the restoration of Thomism was conceived as instrumental to the formation of a new Christian worldview.

Keywords: neo-Thomism, philosophy, theology, nineteenth-century history of thought, Leo XIII

© Valfredo Maria Rossi 2025

ISBNs: 9781009660532 (HB), 9781009660525 (PB), 9781009660563 (OC)
ISSNs: 3033-3954 (online), 3033-3946 (print)

Contents

Introduction	1
1 Thomism and Theological Philosophical Pluralism in the Italian Context before *Aeterni Patris*	3
2 Leo XIII, the Encyclical *Aeterni Patris* and the Revival of Thomism	22
3 The Reception of the Encyclical *Aeterni Patris*: Two Different Interpretative Models	40
Conclusion: From Ideological Thomism to Historical Thomism	61
Bibliography	68

Introduction

The dawn of the nineteenth century marked a decline in scholastic philosophy within the European academic landscape. The severe critiques issued by renowned thinkers like Georg Wilhelm F. Hegel (1770–1831) in Germany and Victor Cousin (1792–1867) in France dealt a significant blow to Scholasticism, which had thrived since the thirteenth century and had been a dominant intellectual movement in subsequent centuries. According to Hegel, Scholasticism is not philosophy, but essentially theology and should be regarded as such. He argued that the Middle Ages did not distinguish between the two disciplines, and their separation marked the transition to modernity when reason began to assert its independence from ecclesiastical theological doctrine.[1] Similarly, Cousin posited that philosophy and theology were intrinsically unified before their separation by René Descartes (1596–1650), often considered the father of modern philosophy.[2] Consequently, the Medieval era is often regarded as a transitional period between Greek and modern philosophy. During this period, philosophical thought was considered to be uniform and insignificant, largely overshadowed by theological understanding. The study of medieval philosophy did not experience a resurgence until the early twentieth century. This renewal was primarily driven by a renewed interest in Thomism, which served as the driving force behind this revival.

The origins of the Thomistic revival can be traced to the early nineteenth century within the Italian Catholic context. However, its rapid and widespread dissemination throughout the Catholic world owes much to the efforts of Pope Leo XIII, who granted Aquinas a privileged status in his encyclical *Aeterni Patris* (4 August 1879).[3] This document effectively established Thomism as the dominant philosophical framework within the Catholic tradition. *Aeterni Patris* played a central role in the Thomistic renewal, to such an extent that the term neo-Thomism began to be used to refer to both philosophy and theology grounded in the doctrines of Aquinas, as interpreted according to the principles outlined in the encyclical. On the wave of *Aeterni Patris*, numerous Thomistic research centres were founded in the subsequent decades, leading to a proliferation of studies aimed at rediscovering Aquinas' philosophy.[4] However, it is essential to recognise that from its inception, neo-Thomism was not merely a philosophical movement focused on the rediscovery of Aquinas' thought. It also had a pronounced ideological dimension, deeply rooted in the context of intransigent Catholicism. This movement explicitly

---

[1] Hegel, *Lectures*, 37–40. [2] Victor Cousin cited in Gilson, *Le philosophe*, 79–81, 160.
[3] Leo XIII, *Aeterni Patris*. Henceforth, it will be abbreviated in *AP*.
[4] Gilson, *Le Thomisme*; Gilson, *La philosphie*.

sought to restore the ideal of a *societas Christiana* (Christian society) and to defend the political and social agenda associated with it.

The present work aims at examining the context of the Thomistic renewal originated by the Leonine encyclical and analysing its implications, with a twofold aim. Firstly, it aims at demonstrating that *Aeterni Patris* constituted a crucial turning point in the history of Catholic philosophical and theological thought. While, on the one hand, this encyclical validated and rejuvenated Thomism, on the other hand, it marked the end of the pluralism that had characterised both Catholic philosophy and theology until then. Secondly, this research aims at showing that the Thomistic revival, as desired by Leo XIII, was not a neutral scholarly pursuit which was dedicated to the in-depth study of Aquinas' philosophy. Rather it represented an ideological endeavour within the intransigent Catholicism, where the resurgence of Aquinas' philosophy was conceived as instrumental in forging a new Christian *Weltanschauung* (worldview).

It was not until the early twentieth century, particularly the 1910s, that Thomism began to shift away from its traditional ideological constraints. This transformation was largely driven by the influence of Étienne Gilson (1884–1978) and his groundbreaking contributions to Thomistic studies. While firmly grounded in Christian thought, Gilson's work introduced a critical historical and scientific approach to the philosophy of Aquinas, thereby laying the foundation for the modern study of medieval thought.

The present study is divided into three sections. Section 1 provides an overview of the multifaceted landscape of Italian philosophical and theological studies before the publication of *Aeterni Patris*. It aims at showing that, contrary to a common opinion, Thomism was not the predominant philosophical current within the Catholic world. In fact, it was a relatively marginal phenomenon, even within Catholic and ecclesiastical institutions. However, it was precisely within this context that the philosophical and social assumptions upon which the recovery of Thomism would be based first emerged.

Section 2 is devoted to an in-depth examination of *Aeterni Patris*. It offers a detailed analysis of the structure and pivotal themes of the encyclical in order to identify the conceptual underpinnings at its core. By contextualising the text within the context of the Leonine renewal agenda, it is possible to shed new light on the prevailing notion of Thomism that emerges from the document, and both the philosophical and social-political implications of *Aeterni Patris*.

Finally, Section 3 focuses on the initial reception and interpretation of the encyclical within the Catholic context. It examines two prominent contemporary commentaries on *Aeterni Patris*, which, through their contrasting perspectives, elucidate the implications of divergent interpretations of Thomism. The commentaries in question are the works of Giovanni Maria Cornoldi (1822–1892)[5] and Carlo Passaglia (1812–1887).[6] Such a comparison is made possible not only by the contemporaneousness of these two texts and their shared literary genre, namely that of the commentary, but primarily by the fact that Passaglia's commentary can be regarded as a direct response to Cornoldi's work, which, in turn, is to be considered as an official commentary on the *Aeterni Patris* due to its content and proximity to the pontiff's entourage.

Within this framework, it becomes possible to distinguish two interpretative currents that arrive at opposite interpretations of Thomism, and can be defined as *maximalist Thomism* and *relativist Thomism*. The maximalist current, which subsequently became the dominant interpretation, sought to establish Thomistic philosophy as the only foundation of Catholic philosophical and theological thought. In contrast, the relativist current regarded Thomism as one among many expressions of the diverse Catholic tradition, despite the notable and significant influence he exerted.

Although there is an extensive literature on *Aeterni Patris* and the revival of Thomism in the nineteenth century, research which focuses on the immediate reception of the Leonine encyclical lack. Moreover, studies on Cornoldi's and Passaglia's commentaries are nearly non-existent. Some valuable information, albeit fragmentary, on Cornoldi's text is available in Luciano Malusa's work.[7] Furthermore, while Passaglia's monograph is occasionally mentioned in some commentaries on *Aeterni Patris*, a comprehensive study that highlights its originality lacks. Additionally, there is no research that compares these two works in order to grasp the divergent conceptions of Thomism that underpin them.

Therefore, the present study aims at providing a preliminary examination of the various responses that Italian Catholic thought developed immediately after the publication of the Leonine encyclical: namely, in a period when Thomism re-emerged as a philosophical doctrine that had to assert the ideological primacy of the church of Rome, and before that Aquinas' thought was reinterpreted according to the historical and philological principles championed by Gilson.

1 Thomism and Theological Philosophical Pluralism in the Italian Context before *Aeterni Patris*

Before analysing Pope Leo XIII's encyclical *Aeterni Patris*, which calls for the revival of Thomism in both philosophy and theology, it is crucial to understand the cultural landscape that preceded its publication. Only within this

---

[5] Cornoldi, 'La regola filosofica'.   [6] Passaglia, *Sulla dottrina*.   [7] Malusa, *Neotomismo*.

multifaceted context the novelty and far-reaching implications of the Leonine reform can be fully grasped.

This introductory section offers an overview of the multifaceted Italian philosophical and theological environment before *Aeterni Patris*. It highlights that the revival of Thomism in the early nineteenth century was a gradual and difficult process.[8] Therefore, labelling the Catholic intellectual movements of this period as merely neo-Scholastic or neo-Thomistic is both premature and misleading. At that time, Thomism was not a dominant philosophical current but a marginal movement that had nearly faded from Catholic academic circles. It was through the efforts of a dedicated group within the area of the intransigent Catholicism that Aquinas' philosophy was seen as a vital antidote to the errors of modern philosophy and society. As a result, Thomism was promoted and defended as a cornerstone of Catholic thought.

1.1 The Revival of Thomism within the Italian Counter-Revolutionary Context

Paolo Dezza, a prominent scholar of the origins of neo-Thomism, emphasises that the resurgence of Aquinas' philosophy took place in Piacenza at the beginning of the nineteenth century, and was led by Canon Vincenzo Buzzetti (1777–1824), a professor at the city's seminary.[9] It's crucial to note that Buzzetti's advocacy for the revival of Aquinas' philosophy, which he termed 'sound philosophy',[10] occurred within the context of Italy's Catholic counter-revolutionary milieu during the late eighteenth and early nineteenth centuries.[11] Against this backdrop, Buzzetti perceived Aquinas' philosophy as a bulwark against the revolutionary ideology that threatened to upend the religious and social order, which was rooted in Christian principles. It is evident that Aquinas was used for ideological purposes. The objective of Thomistic philosophy and theology is not the pursuit of knowledge for its own sake, but rather the means to face and fight the enemy. Buzzetti's ideological stance also had practical implications, as it led him to advocate for a comprehensive overhaul of seminary *curricula*. He believed that only through a unified programme of study based on a sound Thomistic philosophy, namely a philosophy that radically opposed the influences of sensism and empiricism typical of that time, would it be possible to defend the social order against subversion.

---

[8] For an overview of the Thomistic nineteenth-century revival see Marschler, 'Nineteenth-Century', 359–374.

[9] Dezza, *Alle origini*, 13–27. Concerning the evidence of a revival of Thomism as early as the eighteenth century see Rossi, 'La neoscolastica italiana', 365–391.

[10] Buzzetti, *Institutiones sanae philosophiae*.

[11] On the counter-revolutionary Catholic thought in Italy see Fontana, *La controrivoluzione*; see also Guerci, *Uno spettacolo*.

Notwithstanding the occasional anachronistic interpretations of Thomism evident in the work of Buzzetti, such as the defence of the Ptolemaic theory in astronomy on the basis of Aquinas' teaching,[12] it is important to stress that the revival of Thomism was undertaken with the specific purpose of defending the established social order ordained by God against the threats of modernity. Thus, against this apologetic backdrop, Thomistic philosophy emerged as an effective antidote to the dangers of modern thought.

Although Buzzetti's Thomism diverged from the philosophical and theological mainstream of his time, thus causing astonishment and controversy among his contemporaries,[13] it had a significant and enduring impact on some of his disciples, notably the Sordi brothers, Domenico (1790–1880) and Serafino (1793–1865). Both brothers joined the recently re-established Society of Jesus,[14] where they continued to promote Thomistic ideas, although they encountered resistance from within the Jesuit order.

Of the two brothers, Serafino exerted considerable influence in advancing and disseminating Thomistic principles,[15] to such an extent that, according to Dezza, he can be considered the custodian of Buzzetti's intellectual legacy.[16] Serafino's Thomism was characterised by a staunch and uncompromising stance: rather than merely reiterating the doctrines of Aquinas, he sought to reinterpret Thomistic principles in order to address the exigencies of contemporary society and to defend them against the dominant rationalist theories and philosophical systems of his time.[17] As Dezza notes, Serafino Sordi's methodology entailed a comparison between the doctrine of Aquinas and various modern philosophical systems. After elucidating Aquinas's doctrine and substantiating his thesis, Sordi proceeded to compare it with the aforementioned systems, thereby demonstrating the superiority of the former over the latter.[18]

Following Buzzetti's perspectives, Sordi asserts that a sound philosophical system, that is Thomism, is essential to counter the spread of modern errors that challenge the divine socio-political order. This ideological Thomism exerted significant influence both within and beyond the Society of Jesus, largely due to Serafino's extended tenure in the teaching of scholastic philosophy in Jesuit institutions and his prominent roles within the Order.[19]

The person who derived the greatest benefit from Serafino's influence was the Jesuit Luigi Taparelli d'Azeglio (1793–1862). Taparelli's correspondence with

---

[12] Fontana, 'Vincenzo Buzzetti'.   [13] Masnovo, 'Il discorso commemorativo', 160.
[14] Following the suppression of the Society in 1773 with the apostolic brief *Dominus ac Redemptor* by Clement XIV, the Jesuits were re-established on a global scale in 1814 by Pius VII with the bull *Sollicitudo omnium*.
[15] On Serafino Sordi see Dezza, *Alle origini*, 29–64.   [16] Dezza, *Alle origini*, 29.
[17] See Dezza, *Alle origini*, 46.   [18] Dezza, *Alle origini*, 42–43.
[19] Dezza, *Alle origini*, 48–49.

Serafino provides evidence of his significant intellectual evolution towards Thomism.[20] Despite having received an education that included the study of empiricism and eclecticism, which were taught in Jesuit colleges, Taparelli's engagement with Serafino's writings prompted a reorientation towards scholastic philosophy, particularly the teachings of Aquinas. Before this intellectual shift, Taparelli confessed that he had despised Thomism, and thus he began to redo his philosophical training according to the peripatetic method.[21] Taparelli acknowledged Serafino as his mentor and professed to be his loyal disciple.[22] He considered Serafino's works to be fundamental to his study and propagation of Thomism. It is noteworthy that under the guidance of Sordi, Taparelli produced a manuscript, that can be described as a comprehensive compendium of Thomistic philosophy, in which he provided a summary of the fundamental tenets of this theological and philosophical tradition. Taparelli distributed this enigmatic and, in certain respects, initiatory writing in a strictly confidential manner only among those students he deemed most likely to accept this doctrine, pending a time when it would be feasible to reveal it publicly to all.[23] It can thus be observed that, particularly within the context of the Jesuit order and colleges, Thomism still remains a marginal and minority movement that is not held in high esteem. This scarce consideration of Thomism can be attributed to the perception that it was the product of an obsolete philosophical tradition that was no longer capable of adequately explaining the complexities of the modern world.

Taparelli's conversion to Thomism was completed in 1825, during his tenure as Rector of the Roman College (1824–1829).[24] This event marked a crucial moment in the evolution of philosophical studies within this Jesuit institution, although it encountered resistance from some of the faculty members.

1.1.1 Thomism, Traditionalism and the Restoration of Societas Christiana

In the light of the analysis of the pioneering thinkers who rediscovered Scholastic philosophy and Thomism in the early nineteenth century, several observations emerge. As Sandro Fontana observes, for these thinkers

> the pragmatic concerns of socio-political restoration are deemed to outweigh those of a speculative order. Buzzetti, Sordi and Taparelli, who are rightly regarded as the pioneers of the Thomistic renaissance, consider themselves above all to be champions of a *just cause*, activists of a counter-revolutionary ideology and, in those years, convinced supporters of the ideas of Lamennais.

---

[20] Dezza, *Alle origini*, 49. [21] Dezza, *Alle origini*, 49. [22] Dezza, *Alle origini*, 50.
[23] Dezza, *Alle origini*, 50–52.
[24] Dezza, *Alle origini*, 50. See also Pirri, 'Il p. Taparelli', 59–76.

It is therefore not an exaggeration to state that Thomism, in that time, represented the *Italian version* of traditionalist philosophy.[25]

Fontana's observation regarding the close interconnection between Thomism and Traditionalism may initially appear paradoxical. In contrast to rationalist systems, traditionalism posits that human reason is unable to identify truths, including those pertaining to nature, in the absence of faith. Consequently, this stance may be regarded as an example of fideism. This aspect appears to be in conflict with the principles of Scholasticism and Thomism, which uphold a balanced interplay between faith and reason and assert that human beings can grasp natural truths through reason. It is important to note, however, that traditionalism does not merely seek to create an abstract philosophical system based on the idea of *common sense*, which would seek to combat rationalist systems derived from Cartesianism through speculative means. Rather, such a philosophical approach has significant practical and social implications. Traditionalist philosophers aim at 'demolishing at the root any possibility of conceptual elaboration that does not identify itself with religious belief',[26] in order to restore a socio-political system based on religion. In other words, they aim at re-establishing the model of the *societas christiana* that was undermined by the French Revolution. Against this backdrop, it is illuminating to juxtapose the Italian Thomistic renewal with contemporary French traditionalism. As both tendencies are not merely speculative and intellectual, but also practical in nature, it is evident that, in opposition to the social ills caused by the Revolution and Rationalism, it is necessary to propose the re-establishment of a theoretical system that affirms a total identification and unity between the social order and religion, namely between social principles and religious truths.

In France, given the country's longstanding philosophical and scientific advancements since the sixteenth century, the revival of Scholasticism and Thomism appeared to be an unfeasible answer to the challenges posed by Rationalism and its social implications.[27] Conversely, in Italy, which has historically demonstrated a greater resistance to novel cultural influences, the resurgence of Thomism emerged as a compelling model for social and religious

---

[25] 'Le preoccupazioni d'ordine pragmatico di restaurazione politico-sociale [sono] di gran lunga preponderanti nei confronti di quelle d'ordine speculativo: i vari Buzzetti, Sordi, Taparelli, giustamente considerati tra i pionieri della rinascita tomistica, si sentivano soprattutto dei paladini della *giusta causa*, dei propagandisti dell'ideologia contro-rivoluzionaria e, in quegli anni, convinti assertori del verbo lamennesiano. Per cui, senza timore di compiere eccessive forzature, possiamo dire fin d'ora che il tomismo rappresenta, in quel periodo, la *versione italiana* della filosofia tradizionalista'. Fontana, *La controrivoluzione*, 160–161.

[26] 'Demolire alla radice qualsiasi possibilità di elaborazione concettuale che non si identifichi con il credo religiosa'. Fontana, *La controrivoluzione*, 166.

[27] Fontana, *La controrivoluzione*, 161, 163–167.

restoration. 'In order to achieve the objective of political and cultural restoration, the Italian Ultramontane movement drew upon the philosophical resources at its disposal. Meanwhile, in Europe, alternative approaches were explored which were more aligned with the evolving social and religious context.'[28]

Against this backdrop, it is evident that French counter-revolutionary ideas penetrated Italy, where they underwent a process of adaptation to align with the distinctive socio-cultural context of the Italian environment.[29] It is within this context that the resurgence of Aquinas' thought must be understood. That is, the revival of Thomism that took place within the Italian context of intransigent Catholicism in the early nineteenth century was aimed at re-establishing a new social order through the restoration of a unified philosophical paradigm in which all elements were to be harmonised. In this idealised vision of society, reason was to be reconciled with faith, nature with the supernatural, and, notably, the state with the church. Only through such a reconciliation could the medieval *societas christiana* be reconstituted.

1.1.2 The Case of Gioacchino Ventura

Father Gioacchino Ventura (1792–1861) represents a pivotal figure in the convergence between French traditionalism and Italian Thomism, given his status as both a disciple of Lamennais and a staunch Thomist. In his work, *De methodo philosophandi*, Ventura presents a synthesis between the tenets of *common sense* theory and the principles of scholastic Thomistic philosophy. His central thesis reflects the ideas of Catholic counter-revolutionaries, namely, that erroneous philosophies have caused contemporary social turmoil, thus corrupting both human understanding and moral principles.[30] According to Ventura, these false philosophies, stemming from the Protestant heresy, abandon the principle of *common sense* in favour of a *private sense*, that is a subjective interpretation based on the individual reasoning, which is devoid of any rules and any authoritative guidance. The consequence of this approach is the rise of rationalism, which aims at eradicating the experience of faith from society.[31] The rational philosophical method does not aim to explain revealed truths by means of demonstration; rather, it claims to discover truth itself by means of inquiry. The application of this philosophical

---

[28] 'In sostanza, gli ultramontani italiani nel loro disegno di restaurazione politico-culturale utilizzano il materiale filosofico che hanno a disposizione e sul quale si erano *attardati* mentre in Europa venivano tentate vie diverse e più aderenti alla mutata condizione storica'. Fontana, *La controrivoluzione*, 168.

[29] For an analysis of the influence of French counter-revolutionary thought in Italy, see Guerci, *Uno spettacolo*.

[30] Ventura, *De methodo*, III–XVII.   [31] Ventura, *De methodo*, XIII–XVII.

method results in reason becoming the primary criterion for all forms of judgment, thereby leading to the radical rejection of Christianity, which is based on divine revelation.[32] On the contrary, Ventura asserts that sound philosophy must be based on *common sense*, which in turn represents the fundamental principle of Scholastic and Aristotelian philosophy.[33] It is therefore evident that Ventura ascribes contemporary social evils to the perversion of philosophical methodology, thus offering a theological interpretation to the traditionalist argument that modern philosophy has undermined Christian society.[34]

In light of these observations, it is clear that Ventura was indebted to French traditionalism.[35] This debt is so significant that the Catholic journal *Le Corrispondent*, in its review of *De methodo philosophandi*, did not hesitate to state that Ventura had unified 'in a single body of doctrine the philosophical opinions scattered in the writings of De Maistre, De Bonald, De Lammenais and Lurentie'.[36] However, Ventura distinguishes his philosophical approach from that of the aforementioned French thinkers by emphasising the necessity for a comprehensive restoration of a sound philosophical method.[37] While acknowledging the French traditionalists' role in dismantling the impious rationalism of the late eighteenth century, Ventura argues that their failure to ground themselves in Scholasticism undermines their ability to restore Christian philosophy.[38] In other words, Ventura is convinced that, in addition to the *pars destruens* admirably carried out by the French traditionalists, a *pars construens* which seeks to re-establish a sound philosophy on the principles of Scholasticism and Thomism is necessary. Therefore, the proper restoration of the social order will be possible only on the basis of a correct philosophical method: this, in essence, represents the fundamental idea of Ventura's work.

In Ventura's ideological return to Thomism,[39] the principle of substantial unity of all reality emerges as the linchpin of Aquinas' thought and the cornerstone of all philosophy. Through this principle, Ventura seeks to address the fundamental problem of modern society caused by philosophical rationalism: namely, the rupture between God and the world which has resulted in the subversion of both the cognitive and social orders. By re-establishing these bonds at the ontological level through the principle of substantial unity, Ventura aims to make them intrinsically indissoluble.[40]

---

[32] Ventura, *De methodo*, XLIII–LXXIV.   [33] Ventura, *De methodo*, XLVI–XLVII.
[34] Ventura, *De methodo*, XVIII–XLIII.   [35] Fontana, *La controrivoluzione*, 175–185.
[36] 'In un sol corpo di dottrina le opinioni filosofiche sparse negli scritti dei Signori De Maistre, De Bonald, De Lammenais e Lurentie'. Ventura, *Osservazioni*, 3.
[37] Ventura, *Osservazioni*, 3–4.   [38] Ventura, *Osservazioni*, 4–5.
[39] Fontana, *La controrivoluzione*, 178.
[40] On the principle of substantial unity as the cornerstone of all philosophy see Ventura, *De methodo*, LXXV–CXXVII.

If everything is based on the substantial unity of a material element and a formal one which, despite their diversity, are intimately intertwined and thus inseparable,[41] like the soul and the body, then such a unity must also be the fundament of all knowledge and society. From a philosophical perspective, Ventura argues that authentic knowledge emerges from the indivisible conjunction of faith and reason; while from a social perspective, the precondition for harmonious social relations is the unity between those who exercise authority and those who are subject to it.[42] According to Ventura, social unity manifests across three spheres: family, civil order,[43] and, finally, political order. It is precisely within this latter sphere, that the pinnacle of substantial unity, namely the unity between church and state, is achieved.[44] Thus, in this idealised vision, substantial unity becomes the antidote to autonomous and rationalist tendencies that may threaten social cohesion and divine truth transmitted by God.

> For those who are aware of the subsequent development of official Catholic culture throughout the nineteenth century and beyond, the ingenious and truly enduring aspect of Ventura's combination of Lamennaisian ideology and Thomistic tradition, [is] to be found not so much in the theory of common sense as in the so-called *substantial principle* [i.e. the principle of substantial unity]. In other words, Ventura is the first to grasp the ideological efficacy of this Thomistic principle: which enabled nineteenth-century Catholic culture to perpetuate and disseminate the ultramontane ideology in all its aspects (from the anti-rationalist philosophical ones to the political ones against the autonomy of the modern state) behind the orthodox shield of the authoritative magisterium of Aquinas.[45]

1.2 The *Collegio Romano*: Between Pluralism and Thomistic Uniformity

In 1824, Pope Leo XII, through the pontifical brief *Cum multa in Urbe*, entrusted the Roman College (*Collegio Romano*) to the re-established Society of Jesus. This decision, which encountered resistance from the secular

---

[41] Ventura, *De methodo*, LXXVII, ft. 1.   [42] Ventura, *De methodo*, LXXV–LXXXIV.
[43] Ventura, *De methodo*, LXXXIV–LXXXVI.   [44] Ventura, *De methodo*, LXXXVI–LXXXVII.
[45] 'L'aspetto geniale e veramente durevole, per chi abbia presente la successiva evoluzione della cultura ufficiale cattolica lungo tutto l'800 ed anche oltre, della saldatura operata dal Ventura tra ideologia lamennesiana e tradizione tomistica, non [è] da ricercarsi tanto nella teoria del senso comune quanto nel cosiddetto *principio sostanziale* [ovvero il principio dell'unità sostanziale]. In concreto il Ventura è il primo ad avvertire l'efficacia ideologica della rivalutazione di questo principio tomistico: il quale consentiva veramente alla cultura cattolica dell'800 di perpetuare e diffondere l'ideologia ultramontana in tutte le sue implicanze (da quelle filosofiche antirazionalistiche a quelle politiche contro l'autonomia dello Stato moderno) dietro lo schermo ortodosso dell'autorevole magistero di san Tommaso'. Fontana, *La controrivoluzione*, 178–179.

clergy, represents more than a mere academic handover; rather, it must be understood within the broader context of the Catholic restoration envisioned by Leo XII. In accordance with the papal project, the educational issue emerged as a principal instrument for reaffirming genuine cultural and social hegemony.[46] Within this context, the Jesuits, who were once again tasked with the mission of educating the youth, are to be regarded as the custodians of authentic principles and sound Christian customs that had been lost due to the revolution. As Cinzia Sulas points out, 'the restitution of the Roman College is of great historical significance to the Society of Jesus, forming a crucial part of the process of "restoration" and the acquisition of substantial economic and political influence'.[47]

1.2.1 Luigi Taparelli d'Azeglio's Attempt to Reform the Curriculum of Studies at the Collegio Romano

Upon assuming the role of rector at the Roman College, Taparelli encountered an international and academically advanced teaching staff.[48] However, according to Taparelli, this staff had moved away from scholastic teaching, both in philosophy and theology, towards a sort of Cartesianism with sensist influences.[49]

Taparelli was aware of the necessity to eradicate the diversity of doctrines and teaching methods, which were causing confusion within the College.[50] He considered it vital to come back to a unified scholastic system founded upon common philosophical and theological tenets. Taparelli's tenure as Rector was therefore dedicated to reforming the *curriculum* of studies with the objective of aligning the College with the spirit and rule of the Jesuits.

In a manuscript pamphlet entitled *Osservazioni su gli studi del Collegio Romano* (*Observations on the Studies at the Roman College*), dated 1827, Taparelli addressed the fundamental discrepancy between the original decrees of the Jesuit Constitutions and the current teaching practices. The pamphlet was dedicated to the Provincial Father in view of a general revision of the *ratio studiorum* to be applied in all Jesuit colleges.[51] He argued for a return to the ancient doctrines of the Society in order to establish a uniform teaching background at the Roman College. Taparelli's fundamental idea, then, was to come

---

[46] For an analysis of the role of Christian education as a vehicle for cultural hegemony see Rossi, 'Giovanni Fortunato Zamboni', 145–167.
[47] 'La restituzione del Collegio Romano [ai gesuiti] riguarda l'autorappresentazione storica della Compagnia, questione di prim'ordine durante il processo di "restaurazione" e l'acquisizione [da parte della Compagnia stessa] di un forte potere economico e politico'. Sulas, 'La riforma', 304.
[48] Martina, 'Il Collegio Romano', 669.   [49] Filograssi, 'Teologia', 513.
[50] Pirri, 'Il p. Taparelli', 62.
[51] For an analysis of the *ratio* reform see Bianchini, 'La *Ratio Studiorum*', 325–340.

back to the past, to re-establish a connection between the modern teachings of the college with the traditional teachings of the Society. In other words, Taparelli argued that the new *curriculum* should be rooted in the doctrinal tenets of the Jesuit Constitutions in order to remedy the pluralistic approaches among the academic staff. 'According to Taparelli, the Constitutions had a logical and juridical precedence over the renewal of the *ratio*, and for this reason, as Rector of the Roman College, he proposed to preserve this normative deposit unchanged in its fundamental core.'[52] Taparelli therefore wished to propose, by means of the Constitutions, a synthesis of the doctrines to be taught uniformly in the Roman College.

Against this backdrop, it is clear that for Taparelli, pluralism in teaching was unacceptable as it undermined the unity of doctrine, which, as outlined in the Constitutions, was of paramount importance to the identity of the Society of Jesus.

> The Institute – Taparelli states in his *Osservazioni* – commands that every Jesuit should follow the same doctrine, not only in matters of faith, but, as far as possible, in everything. And it is commanded because it is essentially necessary for the good of the Society and consequently these orders are commanded by necessary and immutable laws. To leave opinions free, therefore, is contrary to the Institute and to the nature of the good of the Society. The Institute immutably determines what the only doctrine is to be. . . .Moreover, it would be impossible to adopt a uniform doctrine suitable for our Institute if we did not accept the doctrines as they are presented to us by the Institute. It is therefore the duty and the necessity of every Jesuit to accept them.[53]

After stressing the principle of doctrinal uniformity, Taparelli, citing the Jesuit Constitutions verbatim, asserts that the prescribed doctrine is the Aristotelian–Thomistic one, which, although overlooked, is the only contender against rationalist systems.[54] Consequently, modern philosophies, which originate from the premise of methodological doubt as the foundation of all inquiry and

---

[52] 'Le costituzioni per Taparelli avevano precedenza logica e giuridica rispetto al rinnovamento della *ratio* e per questo, in qualità di rettore del Collegio Romano, proponeva di custodire questo deposito normativo inalterato nel suo nucleo fondamentale'. Sulas, 'La riforma', 313.

[53] 'L'istituto comanda che nella Compagnia tutti seguano una dottrina medesima, non solo ov'è integrata la fede, ma per quanto è possibile, e in tutto. E lo comanda perché questo è necessario essenzialmente al bene della Compagnia e per conseguenza con leggi necessarie e immutabili. Il lasciar libere le opinioni è dunque contrario all'istituto e alla natura del benessere della compagnia. L'istituto determina immutabilmente quale essere debba questa unica Dottrina. . . . D'altronde sarebbe impossibile adottare una dottrina uniforme e adatta al nostro istituto se non abbracciando le dottrine quali egli ce le presenta. Dunque l'abbracciarle è obbligo del gesuita, e anzi necessità'. Taparelli d'Azeglio, *Osservazioni sugli studi del Collegio Romano*, quoted in Sulas, 'La riforma', 316.

[54] Pirri, 'Il p. Taparelli', 72.

thus espouse rationalism while abandoning the principle of authority, must be countered by a robust philosophy that focuses its reflection on *common sense* and an appropriate use of reason.[55]

During the first years of his tenure as Rector of the Roman College, Taparelli's energetic approach gained the support of Father General Luigi Fortis (1748–1829), an ardent advocate of a return to antiquity and peripatetic philosophy in opposition to modern tendencies. However, Taparelli's situation underwent a significant change with the shift in the General Superior and the Society's leadership, a situation that was further complicated by the opposition from the professors at the *Collegio Romano*. In 1829 he was transferred from Rome to Naples as Provincial Father, a move that was seen as the defeat of the Thomistic system that he had passionately defended and the triumph of the philosophical pluralism advocated by the other professors of the Roman College.[56]

Nevertheless, it is noteworthy that during his tenure at the Roman College, Taparelli made significant contributions to the revival and propagation of Thomistic thought. He exerted considerable influence on many of his students, who, in turn, played a key role in the development of Thomism. A prime example is his influence on the young Gioacchino Pecci (1810–1903), later known as Pope Leo XIII. Under Taparelli's tutelage, Pecci embraced Thomism wholeheartedly, to the extent that in 1829, while still a young man, he was appointed by Taparelli himself as a lecturer in philosophy at the Germanic-Hungarian College. This appointment underlined the convergence of the young prelate's philosophical ideas with those of the Rector.[57]

Finally, with regard to Taparelli's efforts to implement Thomistic reform in the Jesuit academic *curriculum*, attention must be drawn to the challenging Neapolitan period of the former Rector of the *Collegio Romano* (1829–1833). Upon assuming the role of Provincial Father in Naples, Taparelli seized the opportunity to implement his Thomistic reform within the Jesuit student residences. First, he replaced all the professors at the *Collegio Massimo*, the most important Jesuit institution in Naples, with ardent supporters of Thomism. 'With such professors, who were specifically instructed to adhere to the Aquinas' doctrine, and with Taparelli at the head of the Scholasticate, it was inevitable that studies would proceed in the intended direction.'[58] Among these newly appointed professors, Father Domenico Sordi deserves mention for his

---

[55] Sulas, 'La riforma', 322. [56] Pirri, 'Il p. Taparelli', 69–73.
[57] Pirri, 'Il p. Taparelli', 73–75.
[58] 'Con simili professori, messi all'insegnamento col comando preciso di attenersi fedelmente alla dottrina di S. Tommaso, e col Taparelli a capo dello Scolasticato, gli studi dovevano necessariamente avere quell'indirizzo che si era voluto dare'. Dezza, *Alle origini*, 62–63.

ardent defence of Thomism. However, his zeal and somewhat inappropriate methods eventually led not only to his suspension from teaching, but also to Taparelli's own expulsion from Naples, thus halting the progress of the Thomistic reform.[59] In 1833, Taparelli was forced to move to Sicily. This expulsion underlined once again the resistance of the Society of Jesus to the Thomistic uniformity advocated by Taparelli.[60]

1.2.2 The Reform of the Ratio Studiorum of 1832 and the Struggle for the Promotion of Thomism

Although Taparelli's departure from the Roman College initially appeared to impede the dissemination of the Aristotelian–Thomistic system he had so vigorously promoted, subsequent developments proved otherwise. A few years later, in 1832, the revision of the new *Ratio Studiorum* was approved. The revised *Ratio* fully embraced the principles that Taparelli had zealously pursued, albeit with little success, in his reform of the Roman College *curriculum*. The new document not only reaffirmed the fundamental structure of the original *Ratio*, thereby safeguarding the authentic identity of the Society, but also reinstated the scholastic structure of philosophy and theology, establishing Aquinas as the preeminent authority in all Jesuit educational institutions.[61] Furthermore, within this context, Thomistic philosophy was tasked with providing students with the intellectual tools necessary to counter modern rationalist trends. Consequently, in addition to its traditional function of supporting theology, philosophy assumed an inherently apologetic role in combating contemporary errors.[62] The *Ratio* of 1832 unambiguously signalled the triumph of the Taparellian approach and set the stage for a process that, within a few decades, would culminate in the dissolution of the philosophical-theological pluralism that had hitherto characterised academic discourse in Jesuit colleges.

In light of this reform, the tensions within the Roman College intensified. While Thomism was gradually promoted from above, primarily through directives from the Jesuit leadership and semi-institutional channels like the journal *La Civiltà Cattolica*, it was met with strong and consistent opposition from the majority of professors at the Roman College, who rejected the Aristotelian–Thomistic framework imposed by the Society government.

Towards the end of the 1850s, there was a resurgence of efforts to establish uniformity in Aristotelian–Thomistic teaching within the Jesuit order. In 1858, Father General Pierre-Jean Beckx (1795–1887) published a significant document, the *Ordinatio pro Triennali Philosophiae Studio*.[63] This work is regarded as one

---

[59] Dezza, *Alle origini*, 63.   [60] Masnovo, *Il neo-tomismo*, 87.   [61] Filograssi, 'Teologia', 515.
[62] Bianchini, 'La *Ratio Studiorum*', 336.   [63] Pachtler and Duhr, *Ratio studiorum*, 555–576.

of the most significant documents on sacred studies prior to Leo XIII's encyclical *Aeterni Patris* and constituted the basis for the subsequent Leonine reform.[64] The *Ordinatio* implemented a rigorous Thomistic reform that effectively prohibited the introduction or retention of alternative philosophical systems in the context of teaching. Aquinas' doctrine was established as the sole authority,[65] and a list of forbidden propositions was drawn up, indicating those not to be taught in the scholasticates of the Society of Jesus. In essence, a kind of *syllabus errorum* was composed with the purpose of condemning all philosophical errors.[66] In particular, ontologism, sensism, idealism, traditionalism and positivism – in other words, all those doctrines that constituted the spectrum of modern philosophy since Descartes – were expressly denounced.[67] Thus, for the first time in an official Jesuit document, the teaching of hylomorphism was mandated, leaving no room for alternative philosophical perspectives and firmly establishing philosophical-theological uniformity.

Despite the authority of this document, a number of professors at the Roman College continued to teach philosophical doctrines that deviated from the Aristotelian–Thomistic framework. In particular, in the scientific and philosophical field, figures such as Fathers Angelo Secchi (1818–1878), Salvatore Tongiorgi (1820–1865), and Domenico Palmieri (1829–1909) not only advocated atomistic and mechanistic theories, but also openly contested hylomorphism, which they considered incompatible with contemporary science and thought.[68] In doing so, they openly contravened the doctrinal guidelines laid down by the Father General. Although the ensuing controversy was intense, it is important to note that these professors should not be labelled as staunch anti-scholastics, defending modern philosophical doctrines in opposition to Scholasticism. Rather, they should be regarded as eclectic thinkers who sought

---

[64] Pirri, 'Intorno alle origini', 410.   [65] Pachtler and Duhr, *Ratio studiorum*, 578.
[66] Concerning the earliest origins of the *Syllabus Errorum*, contemporary historiography generally acknowledges that the initial idea of condemning modern errors was first articulated at the Synod of Spoleto, a regional diocesan synod held in 1849 (see Sandoni, *Il Sillabo*, 26–27). In this context, as Luca Sandoni observes in his seminal work on the genesis of the *Syllabus*, particular attention must be given to the pivotal role played by Gioacchino Pecci, then Bishop of Perugia. For this reason, the initiative to collect and formally denounce modern errors has frequently been ascribed to Pecci's personal initiative, leading some to regard him as the very first architect of the *Syllabus*. However, as Sandoni cautions, 'his interpretation has never been substantiated by solid historical evidence. In fact, it is likely that Pecci's role was exaggerated after his election to the papacy, in an effort to retroactively attribute one of his predecessor's most emblematic acts to him. Such a move would have served to reinforce the sense of continuity between the two pontificates'. ('Questa interpretazione non è però mai stata adeguatamente comprovata in sede storica ed è anzi probabile che il ruolo di Pecci sia stato eccessivamente sottolineato dopo la sua ascesa al soglio pontificio con l'intento apologetico di far risalire al nuovo papa uno degli atti più importanti del suo predecessore, rafforzando così il senso di continuità tra i due pontificati'.) Sandoni, *Il Sillabo*, 27.
[67] Pachtler and Duhr, *Ratio studiorum*, 567–573.   [68] Filograssi, 'Teologia', 516.

to reinterpret traditional philosophical principles within a Christian context, taking into account scientific advances and discoveries. The debate primarily focused on the hylomorphic theory and the resurgence of a rigid Thomism, which was perceived as antiquated and anti-scientific, without undermining those philosophical principles deemed to be doctrinally sound.[69]

Despite several efforts to enforce Thomism, the Roman College remained a stronghold of methodological pluralism until the philosophical reform initiated by Leo XIII. Through his encyclical *Aeterni Patris*, Leo XIII ultimately succeeded in advancing Thomism, even going so far as to replace – or more accurately, purge – nearly the entire teaching staff of the Gregorian University (formerly the Roman College) to guarantee full compliance with the new Thomisitc directives.[70]

1.2.3 The Case of the Roman School

Even within the field of theology, the Roman College demonstrated a notable divergence from the radical Thomism that was gaining prominence during the nineteenth century. In the 1930s, Heribert Schauf coined the term 'Roman School' to describe this distinctive theological approach, which has since become a common topic of discussion in theological circles.[71] Upon analysing the work of some of the theologians who were active at the Roman College between the first and second half of the nineteenth century, Schauf identified a shift away from the conventional tenets of Thomistic Scholasticism in their theological approach.

The term Roman School is primarily associated with four notable Jesuit theologians: namely, Giovanni Perrone (1794–1876), Carlo Passaglia (1812–1887), Clemens Schrader (1820–1875), and Johann Baptist Franzelin (1816–1886). Furthermore, their disciples, including Matthias Joseph Scheeben (1835–1888), who to some extent perpetuated the theological approach learned at the Roman College, can be included in this categorisation.[72] It is important to note that the term 'school' in this context should not be interpreted in the strict sense of a consciously organised and homogeneous group advocating a distinct theological position. Such an approach would fail to capture the nuances of this

---

[69] Filograssi, 'Teologia', 520.
[70] The case of Palmieri, a vehement opponent of Thomism, who was removed from his position at the Roman College in 1878, serves to illustrate this point: Malusa, *Neotomismo*, vol. 1, 278–279. For a broader account of the influence of Leo XIII's reform on the Jesuits of the Roman College, see also Rafferty, 'The Thomistic Revival', 746–773.
[71] Schauf, 'Carl Passaglia', 5; Kasper, *Die Lehre*, 59–77.
[72] For an analysis of the dissemination of Roman School theology throughout Europe, see Shea, '*Ressourcement*', 579–613. On the Roman School see also Levering and Pidel, *The Roman School*.

theological movement. Instead, if viewed in a broader sense, as a theological movement centred on the teachings of select professors who shared certain commonalities but diverged significantly in methodology and content, the term can be seen to retain its validity.

The defining features of theologians of the Roman School are their eclectic approach and their use of positive theology. In contrast to the deductive and syllogistic methodology characteristic of Scholasticism, positive theology emphasises a comprehensive and rigorous examination of theological sources, namely Sacred Scripture and the church's Tradition, which are perceived as dynamic and evolving over time.[73]

This theological perspective has significant implications. If tradition is to be regarded as an organic and vital element then it must be considered in its totality and complexity in order to grasp the truths it contains. Consequently, the theologian who studies revelation in a positive way cannot make any absolute judgements about any particular period or, even less, any individual. In light of the aforementioned considerations, it becomes evident that the theologians of the Roman School do not espouse the absolutisation of Scholasticism or the elevation of Aquinas and his doctrines to the status of an exclusive theological authority. While acknowledging the significance of Scholasticism and Aquinas, they emphasise the need to integrate insights from the Fathers of the church, Scholastics, and subsequent theologians who have enriched the church's Tradition.[74] Thus, the theological methodology of the Roman School endeavours to synthesise diverse elements of the church's living tradition, of which Scholasticism and Aquinas form only a part.

Moreover, as theology is regarded as a science with the objective of rationally investigating revealed truths, theologians are required to engage with their sources in a critical manner and to adopt rigorous research methodologies.[75] This aspect requires scholars to be meticulous in their scholarship, employing a range of scientific tools, including philology, critical analysis, hermeneutics, archaeology, history, and linguistic skills, to elucidate and articulate the truths contained within the sources under scrutiny.[76] In other words, the task of theologian extends beyond mere syllogistic speculation; it

---

[73] On the concept and use of positive theology see Congar, *A History of Theology*, 170–175, 187–190, 227–242. On the theological method of the 'Roman School' theologians see Carola, *Engaging*.

[74] Perrone, *Praelectiones*, § 335–479, pp. 243–340; Passaglia, *De immaculato*, § 1744–1752, pp. 1972–1986.

[75] Perrone, *Praelectiones*, § 335–366, pp. 593–616; Passaglia and Schrader, 'Editorum Praefatio', I–LIV.

[76] Passaglia and Schrader, 'Editorum Praefatio', LII.

encompasses the undertaking of rigorous scientific inquiry into the sources of theological investigation.

In conclusion, the theologians of the Roman School, presented a theology with apologetic and conservative undertones on occasion, but diverged from the rigid Thomism that would later dominate theological discourse in the Catholic world. Instead, their theological approach, rooted in positive theology and a dynamic understanding of tradition, reflected the influences of prominent European theologians such as Johann Adam Möhler (1796–1838) and John Henry Newman (1801–1890).[77] Consequently, it is possible to state that the theologians of the Roman School operated within an international context, receptive to diverse theological methodologies and distinguished by a meticulous examination of sources. Against this backdrop, it can be stated that the four theologians of the Roman College occupy a significant position within the theological and historical discourse of the church. They initiated a reorientation towards the ethos of the inaugural Christian centuries, characterised by a more profound and vibrant form of Christianity, and a positive theology. They represent the genesis of a profound spiritual deepening and the renewal of mystical and liturgical life, of which we are the contemporary witnesses.[78]

1.3 The First Writers of *La Civiltà Cattolica*: Thomism at the Service of Intransigence

On 9 January 1850, the Jesuit journal *La Civiltà Cattolica* was established in Naples amidst numerous challenges, at the explicit request of Pope Pius IX.[79] The journal's objective was to examine significant social, political, and philosophical issues through the lens of Catholic doctrine. Consequently, the journal was intended to serve as a tool for the Pope and the church, with the aim of preserving and disseminating authentic Catholic principles at a time when the church was gradually losing its pivotal role as the leader of society.[80] In essence, *La Civiltà Cattolica* can be seen as an attempt to reaffirm a form of Catholic

---

[77] Giovagnoli, *Dalla teologia*, 31–44; Shea, *Newman's*; Carola, *Engaging*.

[78] Kerkvoorde, 'La théologie', 1030.

[79] On the prodromes and origins of *La Civiltà Cattolica* during the years 1848–1850, as well as the concerns of the Superior General of the Jesuits regarding the establishment of a journal dedicated to such matters, see De Rosa, 'Introduzione', 9–20. Furthermore, it is pertinent to mention that the editorial office of the journal was relocated from Naples to Rome in September 1850. For further details regarding the circumstances surrounding this move, see De Rosa, 'Introduzione', 33–37.

[80] Curci, 'Il giornalismo moderno', 5–24. This initial article, ascribed to Curci (1809–1891), can be regarded as a genuine manifesto of the periodical. It is noteworthy that until 1933, the authors of *La Civiltà Cattolica* remained anonymous. For further details regarding the attribution of the article to Curci see del Chiaro, *Indice*, 50.

cultural hegemony in society, through its meticulous outreach to Catholic communities. As Gabriele De Rosa observes, the journal's pages offer a unique opportunity to trace the evolution of ideas concerning the church's core issues, set against the backdrop of modern society, the philosophies emerging from the liberal revolution, and the new national identity shaped by the *Risorgimento* uprisings.[81]

The close relationship between the journal and the Pope, along with his teachings, is further substantiated by Pius IX's Brief *Gravissimum supremi* of 1866. In this document, issued sixteen years after the foundation of the journal, the Pope definitively established 'the College of Writers of *La Civiltà Cattolica*' (*Il collegio degli scrittori de La Civiltà Cattolica*). This college, similar to other Jesuit institutions, was endowed with its own legal autonomy, enabling the journal's editors to devote themselves exclusively to the defence of Catholicism and the Holy See.[82] The objective of the Pope was to establish a dedicated group of Jesuits, committed solely to the cause of Catholic journalism, which would serve as a powerful platform for disseminating the teachings of the Holy See and Christian doctrine. In other words, just as the numerous Jesuit colleges were tasked with the education of their students, 'the College of Writers of *La Civiltà Cattolica*' was tasked with a broader mission: the shaping of the consciences of all Christians. Against this backdrop, it is evident why the Jesuit journal rapidly acquired recognition as the unofficial mouthpiece of the Holy See and the authoritative interpreter of papal positions.

The inaugural editorial team of the new periodical, which included Father Taparelli, who had been recalled from Sicily to assume this role, was predominantly comprised of ardent Thomists.[83]

Since its foundation, *La Civiltà Cattolica* has consistently advocated for the revitalisation of Christian philosophy in opposition to modern rationalist philosophies. It is important to note, however, that a comprehensive programme for the restoration of Thomism did not emerge until 1853. Despite this, the influence of Aquinas was still present in these early years. As Amato Masnovo observes, 'there are those who, when confronted with the philosophies of Gioberti and Rosmini, hold in their mind the "contemplations of Aquinas", advocating for their expansion and drawing attention to a productive form of

---

[81] De Rosa, 'Introduzione', 23–33.   [82] Pius IX, *Gravissimum supremi*, 9–10.
[83] The inaugural editorial team comprised Carlo Maria Curci, who served in this capacity until 1853; Luigi Taparelli d'Azeglio; Matteo Liberatore (1810–1892); Antonio Bresciani (1798–1862); and Giovanni Battista Pianciani (1784–1862). The initial three editors constituted the Thomist group of the periodical. In 1852, Father Giuseppe Calvetti (1819–1855), a fervent Thomist, was appointed as the fourth member of the editorial team, succeeding Carlo Maria Curci: Masnovo, *Il neo-tomismo*, 92, 97.

Scholasticism'.[84] In essence, during these first years, there existed a sort of latent Thomism. Even in the programmatic article of 1851, entitled *Le nostre speranze (Our Hopes)*[85] – which outlined the journal's directives for the following three years – there was no mention of the possibility of the journal adopting a specific philosophical or theological system, such as Thomism. Instead, the sole system to be embraced and developed remained the Catholic system, comprehended in its entirety.[86]

In 1853, a significant change occurred in the journal. In the programmatic article for the three-year period '53–'55, titled *Il fatto e il da farsi (What has been already done and What needs to be done)*, attributed to Carlo Maria Curci and published at the end of 1852, the call to focus on the crucial issue of restoring true Christian philosophy in Italy began to gain increasing prominence.[87] Thus, in a series of articles attributed to Taparelli, entitled *Di due filosofie (On Two Philosophies)*, the issue of the renewal of modern philosophy in the light of Scholastic principles was addressed.[88] Through a comprehensive and detailed analysis of the two distinct philosophical approaches – the modern inquisitive and the scholastic demonstrative – Taparelli not only highlighted the incompatibility of modern philosophies with Catholic teachings but also concluded that the only viable and authentic Catholic philosophy was that demonstrative.[89] The Piedmontese Jesuit argued that modern inquisitive philosophy was inadequate because it relied exclusively on doubt and reason, leading to a critical rationalism devoid of principles and conclusions. On the contrary, he proposed that scholastic demonstrative philosophy represented the optimal approach to authentic philosophy, as it could grasp the certainty of principles and the evidence of demonstrations, based on authority and faith.[90]

> We shall therefore demonstrate – Taparelli stated – that the *demonstrative* philosophy of the Scholastic philosophers can be counterposed to modern *inquisitive* philosophy on the basis of four characteristics. Firstly, the former commences with certainty, whereas the latter is grounded in doubt. Secondly, the former's ultimate objective is evidence, whereas the latter's aim is the certainty. Thirdly, the former employs the support of all reasonable elements to reinforce its thesis, whereas the latter accepts only reason. Fourthly, the

---

[84] 'C'è chi di fronte alla filosofia del Gioberti e del Rosmini custodisce nello spirito le 'contemplazioni dell'Aquinate' [...e] ne caldeggia l'incremento e chiama l'attenzione sopra un anonimo e il suo fruttuoso scolasticismo.' Masnovo, *Il neo-tomismo*, 88–89.
[85] Curci, 'Le nostre speranze', 5–16. On the attribution to Curci see del Chiaro, *Indice*, 50.
[86] Curci, 'Le nostre speranze', 14.   [87] Curci, 'Il fatto e il da farsi', 141; Del Chiaro, *Indice*, 51.
[88] Taparelli d'Azeglio, 'Di due filosofie', 369–380, 481–506, 626–647; Del Chiaro, *Indice*, 97.
[89] Taparelli d'Azeglio, 'Di due filosofie', 645–647.
[90] Taparelli d'Azeglio, 'Di due filosofie', 492–506, 626–633.

former instils in souls a Catholic, social, and practical disposition, whereas the latter fosters a heterodox, anti-social, and impractical disposition.[91]

In 1853, a new article was published which placed increasing emphasis on the necessity of reclaiming medieval philosophy, particularly that of Aquinas, in order to counter the prevailing philosophical chaos of the modern era. The article, entitled *Del progresso filosofico possibile nel tempo presente* (*On the Possible Philosophical Progress in the Present Time*) and attributed to Giuseppe Calvetti, provided a strong argument for why Aquinas' philosophy, when reinterpreted in the context of contemporary social issues, should serve as the cornerstone of Christian philosophy.[92] Aquinas was thus lauded as the indisputable authority and reliable guide in the field of philosophy.[93] Consequently, if Catholic philosophy was to remain unwavering in its commitment to truth and avoid being unduly influenced by modern errors, it was essential to revive Thomism and anchor its principles in Aquinas' teachings. With the publication of Calvetti's article in *La Civiltà Cattolica*, the intentions of the journal became apparent. The idea of restoring Christian philosophy, which had been discussed in a general sense from the outset, was now linked to the revival of Thomism.[94] Aquinas' philosophy was therefore presented as the embodiment of the entire Catholic system: the combination of Thomism and Christian philosophy, along with the resulting interpretative reductionism, was now complete.

It is evident that, while there was a common desire among the Jesuits of *La Civiltà Cattolica* to revive Aquinas' thought and covertly re-establish Thomism until 1852, by 1855 there was a clear awareness of having commenced this restoration and having laid the foundations for its realisation. This would be accomplished in the following years.[95] Over the subsequent decades, *La Civiltà Cattolica* assiduously propagated Thomism, establishing it as the theoretical foundation and interpretive framework for a variety of subjects. As a result, Aquinas' doctrines were not only applied to philosophy but also extended and adapted to sociological, political, and even economic contexts.[96] This process

---

[91] 'Mostreremo dunque che la filosofia degli Scolastici può come *dimostrativa* contrapporsi alla moderna *inquisitiva* per quattro sue proprietà: vale a dire perché: 1. Quella moveva dal certo, questa dal dubbio: 2. *Proprio* scopo di quella era l'evidenza, di questa la certezza: 3. Quella per *accertare* nelle sue sentenze invocava a sostegno qualsivoglia elemento ragionevole, questa ne accetta solo uno, il raziocinio: 4. Quella produceva negli animi una disposizione cattolica, sociale, pratica; questa una disposizione eterodossa antisociale impraticabile'. Taparelli d'Azeglio, 'Di due filosofie', 378.

[92] Calvetti, 'Del progresso filosofico', 265–287. Del Chiaro, *Indice*, 97.

[93] Calvetti, 'Del progresso filosofico', 270.

[94] Taparelli d'Azeglio, 'Terza serie', 615; Del Chiaro, *Indice*, 51.

[95] Masnovo, *Il neo-tomismo*, 100.

[96] De Rosa, 'Introduzione', 54–55. On this point see also Masnovo, *Il neo-tomismo*, 113–117.

fostered the development of a distinctly Thomistic worldview, which increasingly influenced Catholic thought throughout that period.

> This marks the beginning of the integration of Thomism with the interpretation of contemporary social and political developments (which were perceived as unfavourable to Catholicism and the Church). Speculative reflection was to provide criteria and instruments for strengthening the doctrinal and operational unity of Catholics and for reconstructing a hierocratic society. The proposed model of society is that of a civil consortium based on adherence to Catholic principles proclaimed by the ecclesiastical magisterium. It is characterised by the recognition of the sacred dimension of political power, exemplified by the unity of powers inherent in the monarch, and is in opposition to any evolution of orders toward a constitutional and representative framework.[97]

In conclusion, it can be affirmed that the efforts of the Jesuits at *La Civiltà Cattolica* played a pivotal role in the development of maximalist Thomism between 1850 and 1870. This approach to Thomism aimed to permeate every aspect of Catholic thought, effectively closing off any room for alternative viewpoints. This intellectual framework would provide the foundation for Leo XIII's reform initiatives, and, beginning in the late 1870s with the encyclical *Aeterni Patris*, it would ultimately seal the triumph of Thomism within the church.

2 Leo XIII, the Encyclical *Aeterni Patris* and the Revival of Thomism

As discussed in the Section 1, the philosophical and theological landscape that preceded the Thomistic revival of the late nineteenth century led by Pope Leo XIII, was marked by cultural pluralism and the gradual, often challenging, resurgence of Thomism. This revival was particularly intertwined with Catholic counter-revolutionary circles, where Aquinas' philosophy served ideological and apologetic purposes. Against this background, attention now shifts to the Encyclical *Aeterni Patris*, which represents a pivotal moment in the development of Thomism within the Catholic tradition.

This section is dedicated to analysing the Leonine encyclical. Section 2.1 contextualises *Aeterni Patris* within Leo XIII's broader reformist agenda.

---

[97] 'Cominciava così ad attuarsi quella saldatura tra rinascita del tomismo e interpretazione degli sviluppi sociali e politici contemporanei (intesi come sostanzialmente avversi al cattolicesimo e alla Chiesa) a cui la riflessione speculativa avrebbe dovuto apportare criteri e strumenti per rafforzare l'unità dottrinale e operativa dei cattolici e ricostruire una società di tipo ierocratico: un modello di consorzio civile caratterizzato dall'adesione ai principi cattolici enunciati dal magistero ecclesiastico e fondato sul riconoscimento della dimensione sacrale del potere politico, ben rappresentato nell'unità dei poteri tipica del monarca, contro ogni evoluzione degli ordinamenti in chiave costituzionale e rappresentativa'. Vian, 'Luigi Taparelli d'Azeglio'.

Section 2.2 provides a detailed examination of the encyclical's structure and content, focusing on the key milestones in Leonine philosophical reform. Finally, Section 2.3 explores the significant socio-political implications of the philosophical approach outlined in the encyclical.

2.1 *Inscrutabili Dei consilio*: The Programmatic Encyclical of Leo XIII's Pontificate

In order to gain a deeper understanding of the profound implications embedded within *Aeterni Patris*, it is necessary to undertake a closer examination of an earlier document by Leo XIII, namely the encyclical *Inscrutabili Dei consilio*, published on 21 April 1878. As Pope Leo's inaugural encyclical, it functions as a programmatic text, articulating the fundamental tenets that would guide his pontificate. It is therefore an indispensable text for understanding the subsequent philosophical reforms articulated in *Aeterni Patris*. Indeed, the close relationship between the two encyclicals, published just over a year apart, suggests that *Aeterni Patris* can be seen as the practical realisation of the agenda outlined in *Inscrutabili Dei consilio*. Thus, *Inscrutabili Dei consilio* can be considered the immediate source of *Aeterni Patris*.[98]

Inscrutabili Dei consilio begins by noting the detrimental impact of social ills that oppress the human race on every side.[99] The pope then proceeds to delineate the causes and consequences of these ills meticulously, before prescribing efficacious remedies for the restoration of social order in accordance with divine will.[100] Leo XIII attributes these evils to the subversion of the God-ordained principles upon which society is founded.

The pontiff posits that the causes of such a social debacle lie in the disdain for the church and the rejection of its divine authority.[101] The church is in fact the bedrock of all order, morality, and justice in both the private and public spheres. Therefore, it must reclaim its rightful hegemonic role in society, a role inherent to its very nature. The development of civil society, the pope continues, is the result of the church's steadfast dedication over centuries, guiding humanity from barbarism to civilisation through its teachings and support of the sciences and arts.[102] Thus, any attempt to suppress the church's authoritative voice in society must be regarded as a regression to the chaos of error and disorder.[103]

---

[98] Silvestrelli, 'Le fonti immediate', 138–140.   [99] *Inscrutabili Dei*, n. 2.
[100] The Latin title of the encyclical is clarifying in this regard: 'Epistola Encyclica ad Episcopos universos catholici Orbis, de malis humanae societatis, eorum causis et remediis'. ('Encyclical letter to all catholic bishops on the evils of human society and their causes and remedies'.) Leo XIII, *Allocutiones*, 5.
[101] *Inscrutabili Dei*, n. 3.   [102] *Inscrutabili Dei*, n. 5.   [103] *Inscrutabili Dei*, n. 6.

Furthermore, *Inscrutabili Dei consilio* identifies two pivotal elements through which the church is tasked with fulfilling its role as the leader of society:[104] temporal power and the education of youth. These elements are considered essential remedies for restoring society to its rightful order and consolidating it on a Christian foundation.

Setting aside the first aspect – namely, the vindication of temporal power, deemed necessary for the church to freely exercise its influence – [105] the second aspect, which pertains to education, will now be examined. It is precisely this second element that will form the conceptual foundation of the encyclical *Aeterni Patris*.

Addressing the bishops, Leo XIII exhorts them to 'kindle the fire of the love of religion among the faithful' through their actions.[106] Although this address seems to be a pastoral appeal, it has profound philosophical and social implications. By citing Colossians 2:8 ('beware lest any man cheat you by philosophy and vain deceit'), the encyclical associates the development of 'the current errors' with the propagation of false philosophies.[107] Thus, as a remedy to this decline, the encyclical emphasises the necessity for an education that is to be grounded in sound Christian principles, and a philosophical method that is to be firmly rooted in the faith of the church. In other words, it advocates for a philosophy that, in conformity with divine revelation, can accurately explore divine and human principles while also defending the faith against adversaries.

> The more the enemies of religion exert themselves to offer the uninformed, especially the young, such instruction as darkens the mind and corrupts morals, the more actively should we endeavor that not only a suitable and solid method of education may flourish but above all that this education be wholly in harmony with the Catholic faith in its literature and system of training, and chiefly in philosophy, upon which the direction of other sciences in great measure depends. Philosophy seeks not the overthrow of divine revelation, but delights rather to prepare its way, and defend it against assailants, both by example and in written works, as the great Augustine and the Angelic Doctor, with all other teachers of Christian wisdom, have proved to Us.[108]

The close correlation between philosophy and faith, as reaffirmed by the papal document, has significant implications. Although the encyclical addresses a philosophical issue in the field of education, which traditionally falls outside the church's magisterium, which in turn deals exclusively with matters of faith

---

[104] On the social function of the church see also Liberatore, 'L'enciclica', 645. On the attribution of the article to Liberatore see del Chiaro, *Indice*, 144.
[105] *Inscrutabili Dei*, n. 12.   [106] *Inscrutabili Dei*, n. 13.   [107] *Inscrutabili Dei*, n. 13.
[108] *Inscrutabili Dei*, n. 13.

and morals, it nevertheless asserts that if philosophy is understood as a discipline contingent on faith and if faith is safeguarded and regulated by the church, then even philosophy must fall under the authority of the church. The church thus begins to extend its magisterium even to philosophy, given that the defence of the fundamental moral and social values depends on a correct philosophical approach.

In light of these considerations, it becomes evident that Leo XIII's programmatic encyclical represents an attempt to establish a unified system of thought capable of addressing the multifaceted challenges posed by modern society. These challenges encompass religious, philosophical, cultural, political, and social domains. The subsequent Leonine encyclical, *Aeterni Patris*, is wholly devoted to the question of the necessity of a sound Christian philosophy, thereby providing a concrete manifestation of this approach.

2.2 The *Aeterni Patris*: Structure and Content

On 4 August 1879, the Leonine encyclical *Aeterni Patris*, which addresses the renewal of philosophy within the Christian sphere, was officially published. This encyclical represents a pivotal moment in the history of Catholic studies. It not only consolidated the Thomistic renewal movement, which had been gradually shaping the Catholic world since the early nineteenth century, but also established conceptual and practical guidelines. These recommendations influenced subsequent developments in philosophical studies and gave shape to a unified Thomistic thought, thereby providing an interpretative framework through which all reality could be understood.

Although the encyclical is presented as a single text without internal subdivisions, a closer examination reveals that it is structured around three key themes, which form three thematic units. These units are preceded by a general introduction, which is necessary to contextualise the cultural climate in which the encyclical is situated.[109] The initial section explores the characteristics of true philosophy,[110] whereas the subsequent section offers a historical overview, emphasising the significance and centrality of Aquinas.[111] In conclusion, the text presents a third section which addresses the subject of false philosophy and the necessary measures to be taken against it.[112]

Prior to undertaking a comprehensive examination of the papal document, it is essential to briefly consider the significance of its title. The title explicitly summarises the ultimate aim of the Leonine writing: 'On the Christian philosophy to be established in Catholic schools in accordance with the thought of

---

[109] *AP*, n. 1–2.   [110] *AP*, n. 3–9.   [111] *AP*, n. 10–23.   [112] *AP*, n. 24–34.

St. Thomas Aquinas.'[113] While this incipit is not present in the first edition of the encyclical published in *Acta Sanctae Sedis*,[114] it was incorporated from the outset, and became an integral part of the official text.[115]

2.2.1 Introduction

Before delving into the analysis of modern times and more philosophical issues, the encyclical opens by reaffirming the immutable essence of the church, the means by which it operates, and the end to which it tends. Although these arguments may initially appear unrelated to the central theme of the encyclical, they actually serve as the essential ecclesiological foundations upon which the entire document is built and justified.

The church, in accordance with its institution by Christ, is described as the 'the common and supreme teacher of the peoples'.[116] Consequently, the church is called to act in accordance with its nature, which requires it to 'train the minds to faith, ...teach religion and contend forever against errors'.[117] In other words, the church, through its unfailing magisterium, must necessarily guide the whole of society to ensure its growth and development in accordance with the divine order.

Once the nature and mission of the church have been established, the encyclical proceeds to examine the close connection between philosophy and faith, echoing arguments previously articulated in *Inscrutabili Dei consilio*:

> Since, then, according to the warning of the apostle, the minds of Christ's faithful are apt to be deceived and the integrity of the faith to be corrupted among men by philosophy and vain deceit, the supreme pastors of the Church have always thought it their duty to advance, by every means in their power, science truly so called, and at the same time to provide with special care that all studies should accord with the Catholic faith, especially philosophy, on which a right interpretation of the other sciences in great part depends.... But now, both by reason of the gravity of the subject and the condition of the time, we are again compelled to speak to you on the mode of taking up the study of philosophy which shall respond most fitly to the excellence of faith, and at the same time be consonant with the dignity of human science.[118]

It can therefore be argued that, while erroneous philosophical teachings may mislead individuals and erode the foundations of religious belief, a robust and well-founded philosophical tradition is regarded as a vital catalyst for the advancement of faith. Consequently, despite being regarded as a secular

---

[113] 'De philophia christiana ad mentem Sancti Thomae Aquinatis in scholis catholicis instauranda'. *AP*.
[114] *Acta Sanctae Sedis in compendium oportune redacta et illustrata*, vol. 12, Romae 1879, 97–115.
[115] Leo XIII, *Acta*, 255.   [116] *AP*, n. 1.   [117] *AP*, n. 1.   [118] *AP*, n. 1.

discipline, philosophy is to be subjected to direct doctrinal guidance from the magisterium of the church.

Aware of the significant implications of a sound philosophical approach, the encyclical proceeds to delineate the contemporary context. The text presents a radically pessimistic view of modern society, which has become adrift as a result of modern philosophical doctrines that have divorced themselves from faith. In a word, these doctrines have misguided and misled the human mind.[119]

In conclusion, the opening pages of the encyclical reveal that the entire document is structured around a coherent conceptual framework: namely, that philosophy and faith are inextricably linked, and that, as a consequence, the former must be subject to the authority of the church's magisterium. The encyclical identifies erroneous philosophy as the root cause of social evils and moral decay, contending that it leads individuals to act without reference to true and immutable principles. Conversely, it maintains that sound philosophy – when in harmony with the tenets of faith – constitutes an indispensable instrument for genuine moral renewal and for the reconstruction of society upon authentically Christian foundations.

In light of the aforementioned introductory lines, it becomes evident that the project of philosophical renewal proposed by *Aeterni Patris* extends well beyond the boundaries of theoretical speculation. That is, the issues at stake cannot be reduced to a mere dispute among competing philosophical schools, with the Pope simply intervening as an authoritative arbiter. Rather, the papal initiative must be understood within the broader framework of a comprehensive programme of social reform, in which philosophical renewal constitutes the indispensable point of departure: namely, reclaiming consciences through proper philosophical education as a means of restoring society. This, in essence, represents the foundational programme articulated by Leo XIII in *Aeterni Patris*.

2.2.2 Part 1: True Philosophy

Having outlined the function of philosophy within the magisterium of the church and identified the fundamental causes of the malaise afflicting modern society, the encyclical proceeds to examine the defining characteristics, responsibilities, and constraints of authentic philosophy.

Given its intrinsic limitations as a human endeavour, philosophy is unable to provide an independent path to truth. Consequently, the attainment of truth is achieved through the act of faith, particularly through the adherence to divine revelation. Therefore, to be effective, philosophy – understood as a natural

---
[119] *AP*, n. 2.

instrumente provided by God to aid in the investigation of truths – must remain closely intertwined with faith. A symbiotic relationship emerges between faith and reason, with each reinforcing and complementing the other. Faith illumines reason, extending its capacity to apprehend truths that transcend the limits of pure rationality, while reason, in turn, provides faith with the logical and argumentative structure necessary for theological discourse to be both intellectually grounded and universally accessible.[120]

Within this paradigm, the essential functions that genuine philosophy must fulfil, as well as the boundaries within which it operates, are delineated.

Tasks of Philosophy

'In the first place, philosophy, if rightly made use of by the wise, in a certain way tends to smooth and fortify the road to true faith, and to prepare the souls of its disciples for the fit reception of revelation.'[121] In essence, the principal aim of genuine philosophy is to serve as a propaedeutic to faith. Consequently, the role of philosophy is to examine and elucidate all natural truths that are fundamental to leading towards the threshold of faith.

In order to fully comprehend this notion, it is essential to delineate the various categories of truth that the encyclical presupposes. There are truths that are purely natural and discernible through rational illumination, namely just through philosophical inquiry. Conversely, there are supernatural truths pertaining to divine matters that are only accessible through divine revelation. Reason alone is inadequate for comprehending or intuiting such truths. Once revealed, however, these truths become subjects of rational inquiry, thus opening the field for theological inquiry. In addition, there are certain truths which, while belonging to the domain of divine revelation, may nonetheless be fully known through sound philosophical inquiry alone. Consequently, these truths intersect both philosophy and natural theology, namely those disciplines capable of deducing certain aspects of God, such as His existence, attributes, and creation of the world, solely through rational speculation.

In the context of philosophy's role as a propaedeutic to faith, the encyclical makes explicit reference to this third category of truths, that is those concerning divine realities which, though belonging to the order of revelation, remain accessible to investigation through the light of natural reason.[122] Two specific truths are highlighted: the existence of God and the attributes ascribed to Him, with a particular focus on the attribute of divine truth.[123] The argument presented in the papal document is that natural reason, and thus philosophy, has the responsibility of establishing the existence of God and His truth for humanity. In

---

[120] *AP*, n. 2. [121] *AP*, n. 4. [122] *AP*, n. 4. [123] *AP*, n. 5.

essence, the objective of philosophy is to facilitate human understanding of the rational knowledge of God and His truths. Once this foundational understanding is established, individuals are prepared to accept divine revelation in its entirety. If people establish the existence and truth of God through rational inquiry, it follows that they must accept divine revelation as truth.

In support of this approach, the encyclical cites the testimony of ancient pagan philosophers, namely those who, prior to the advent of Christ and, therefore, of divine revelation, had investigated and attained these truths solely through rational inquiry. These philosophers, therefore, serve as witnesses to a philosophy that, by paving the way to knowledge of God, can admirably fulfil its propaedeutic role with respect to faith itself. However, the document continues, if, on the one hand, the teaching of such philosophers bears favourable witness to the Christian faith and shows how natural reason alone can arrive at such profound doctrines, on the other hand, it must always be emphasised that such reason is called upon to arrive at even higher and deeper truths. This can only happen when reason is illuminated by divine revelation.[124]

The second function of philosophy is to provide support for theology.[125] Although theology is a discipline that is grounded on revealed truths, it requires an argumentative basis in order to investigate and understand these truths in greater depth. Consequently, philosophy is tasked with providing theology with the necessary instruments to facilitate a rational analysis supported by a scientific method. In light of these assumptions, it can be argued that theology is also a true scientific discipline. Indeed, as the encyclical asserts, theology,

> the most noble of studies, ... requires to bind together, as it were, in one body the many and various parts of the heavenly doctrines, that, each being allotted to its own proper place and derived from its own proper principles, the whole may join together in a complete union; in order, in fine, that all and each part may be strengthened by its own and the others' invincible arguments.[126]

Consequently, philosophy – through the disciplined application of deductive reasoning and argumentation – furnishes theology with the indispensable tools for constructing a rational inquiry into revealed truths. The medieval conception of *philosophia ancilla theologiae* (philosophy as the handmaiden of theology), according to which philosophy is wholly subordinated to theological investigation and demonstration, is thus reaffirmed.

Finally, as a third task, philosophy must also serve an apologetic function: 'the duty of religiously defending the truths divinely delivered, and of resisting those who dare oppose them, pertains to philosophic pursuits'.[127] In light of this consideration, it can be argued that philosophy should be employed as a means

---
[124] *AP*, n. 4. [125] *AP*, n. 6. [126] *AP*, n. 6. [127] *AP*, n. 7.

of both defence and attack. Firstly, it must elucidate and substantiate the rational intelligibility and intrinsic veracity of revealed truths, thereby defending the credibility of revelation. Secondly, it must challenge the theories of those who oppose faith, demonstrating how philosophical arguments can be employed to undermine the reliability and foundations of divine revelation. It is only through this valiant battle, waged with the same weapons as the enemies and on their own ground – namely that of rational investigation, and with the means made available by philosophy – that sound doctrine can be established as true and disseminated among the nations.[128]

In light of these considerations, the ancillary function that genuine philosophy must fulfil, as well as the limits within which it operates, are delineated. Consequently, philosophy is not regarded as an autonomous rational science in and of itself. Rather, it is viewed as a means of attaining, deepening and defending the truths of faith.

Limits of Philosophy

If, as it has been observed, true philosophy is called upon to perform its ancillary function to revealed truths, it follows that it will also have to submit to two very precise limits.

It is clear that the focal point of the entire argumentation on which the encyclical hinges is not philosophy in and of itself, but rather divine revelation. Indeed, it is the latter that imbues philosophy with meaning, rather than the other way around. It is evident that divine revelation, as the work of God, represents the pinnacle of veracity and must be accepted as such. Conversely, philosophy, being a purely human pursuit, is inherently constrained by the limitations of human reasoning. Therefore, philosophical inquiry as such is unable to address the supernatural. It can therefore neither 'deny those truths, nor measure them by its own standard, nor interpret them at will'.[129] It is evident that the first limit of philosophy is precisely divine revelation. Consequently, philosophy must be aware of its own limitations and of the greatness and truth of divine revelation. It must submit to it, accepting it humbly and with faith.[130]

This premise entails a logical consequence: if revelation constitutes the primary limitation of philosophy, it follows that the secondary limit is represented by the authority of the church. This presupposes that the church, by virtue of its nature and constitution, regards itself as the guardian of revelation.

The encyclical develops this concept, reiterating the importance of philosophy always applying its own method of investigation and reflection in natural questions, namely in those questions that can be understood by human

---

[128] *AP*, n. 7.   [129] *AP*, n. 8.   [130] *AP*, n. 8.

intelligence on its own, without the aid of faith. However, this method cannot be employed in an autonomous manner, that is to say, 'in such fashion as to seem rashly to withdraw from the divine authority'.[131] The document's intention is to clarify that the conclusions of a philosopher, even if they pertain to a natural sphere (i.e. one that is not directly related to divine revelation), cannot be in contradiction with the doctrine that has been revealed by the church. It thus follows that, given the church's self-ascribed infallible authority over revelation, the philosopher must be subject to the voice of the church's magisterium, not only with regard to explicitly *de fide* matters, but also with regard to those matters that, although not part of revelation, are nevertheless considered by the magisterium as pertaining to revelation itself.

> For the human mind, being confined within certain limits, and those narrow enough, is exposed to many errors and is ignorant of many things; whereas the Christian faith, reposing on the authority of God, is the unfailing mistress of truth, whom whoso followeth he will be neither enmeshed in the snares of error nor tossed hither and thither on the waves of fluctuating opinion. Those, therefore, who to the study of philosophy unite obedience to the Christian faith, are philosophizing in the best possible way; for the splendor of the divine truths, received into the mind, helps the understanding, and not only detracts in nowise from its dignity, but adds greatly to its nobility, keenness, and stability.[132]

Against this backdrop, it can be argued that a philosophy which is aware of its own limitations and meekly submits to divine revelation and the authority of the church is the only sound philosophy, since it is only through faith that reason is freed from error and enriched with knowledge.

On the basis of these assumptions, the encyclical also addresses the question of the relationship between *fides* and *ratio*. According to *Aeterni Patris*, it is crucial to maintain a reciprocal balance between these two poles; otherwise, the system is at risk of either falling into fideism, in which all autonomy of reason and philosophical inquiry is annulled, or into rationalism, whereby the possibility of all divine revelation and supernatural truth is eliminated on the basis of a pure rationalism that elevates reason to the authority of itself. Consequently, faith cannot be regarded as the enemy of reason, since reason can avoid error and can arrive at the truth safely, precisely thanks to faith.[133]

In conclusion, an analysis of the arguments presented in this opening section reveals that, according to the encyclical, the sole viable philosophical approach is that which is consonant with Christian thought. This entails that the only legitimate philosophy is a Christian one, insofar as it acknowledges its divine origin and remains subject to the authority of the church.

---

[131] *AP*, n. 8.   [132] *AP*, n. 9.   [133] *AP*, n. 9.

2.2.3 Part 2: Historical Excursus and the Greatness of Aquinas

Once the fundamental principles of genuine philosophical discourse have been established, the encyclical proceeds to present a comprehensive historical overview of the ancient philosophers. What may initially seem to be an unnecessarily lengthy digression that disrupts the progression of the argument ultimately proves to be a pivotal element in the document's overall development. Moreover, it is important to note that, although this second section may appear to be a mere historical account, it is in fact driven by an explicitly ideological intent. The digression serves to substantiate the theoretical assertions concerning the nature and characteristics of true philosophy that have been made previously. In other words, the history of philosophy clearly demonstrates that, without faith, philosophy cannot reach the heights to which it is called, and thus becomes lost in error. The most influential philosophers of antiquity bear witness to this:

> The philosophers of old who lacked the gift of faith, yet were esteemed so wise, fell into many appalling errors. You know how often among some truths they taught false and incongruous things; what vague and doubtful opinions they held concerning the nature of the Divinity, the first origin of things, the government of the world, the divine knowledge of the future, the cause and principle of evil, the ultimate end of man, the eternal beatitude, concerning virtue and vice, and other matters, a true and certain knowledge of which is most necessary to the human race.[134]

These philosophers are distinguished from the church Fathers and ecclesiastical doctors, who conducted their philosophical research in accordance with the tenets of faith and divine revelation. This is why they exemplify the actualisation of genuine philosophical discourse, wherein faith and reason are inextricably intertwined.

The initial section of this excursus examines the early church Fathers up to the advent of the Middle Ages; that is, from Justin to Anselm, traversing the works of Irenaeus, Origen, Tertullian, and Augustine.[135] Despite their diversity – encompassing differences of era, culture, language, style, philosophical schools, and the range of issues and themes addressed – they are unified by a common methodology characterised by a harmonious balance between faith and reason. In essence, they stand as concrete exemplars of the excellence of Christian philosophy.[136]

Having mentioned the fathers of antiquity, the encyclical then turns to the doctors of the Middle Ages, namely the scholastics.[137] The latters are regarded as the logical successors and continuators of the work already undertaken by the

---

[134] *AP*, n. 10. [135] *AP*, n. 11–13. [136] *AP*, n. 10. [137] *AP*, n. 14–16.

church Fathers. Indeed, their significance lies in their ability to collect and rework in a systematic manner the ancient doctrine of the church.[138] The scholastics are thus regarded as the great systematisers of doctrinal knowledge. Moreover, they are lauded for their exceptional capacity to integrate faith and reason, rendering them an indivisible entity whose most sophisticated product is theology, at the service of which philosophy is then placed.[139] It is evident that theological reflection represents the pinnacle of human intellectual achievement, insofar as it represents the culmination of a mind that, driven by faith, attains its full potential, namely, the capacity to reflect and argue about God.[140] The logical consequence of these assumptions is that philosophy is relegated to wholly a subordinate role. Indeed, while the encyclical states that scholastic philosophy is to be commended with the same praise as theology, it is regarded as a mere supplement to theological inquiry, serving to provide it with a robust and logical foundation.[141] In light of the aforementioned reasoning, it can be stated that the scholastics are to be regarded as unparalleled experts in this field. By establishing philosophy as the systematic foundation for theology and theology as the science that imbues the other sciences with meaning, they have given rise to a genuine Christian worldview. This worldview is characterised by a profound interconnection between faith and reason, philosophy and theology, and the natural and supernatural dimensions, which are inextricably linked and inseparable.

It can thus be concluded that, in its ancillary role, scholastic philosophy will serve as the model and exemplar for the implementation of the philosophical renewal theorised and desired by Leo XIII, as it encompasses all the characteristics of true philosophy as outlined in the encyclical.

Nevertheless, among the scholastics, Aquinas occupies a unique position, being lauded as 'the chief and master of all [scholastic doctors]'.[142] The historical overview is structured in a continuous ascending climax, culminating in Aquinas' celebration. Aquinas is regarded as the epitome of scholastic philosophy and theology. He collects together the disparate doctrines of other philosophers into an organic system. This systematic approach enables him to grasp an unattainable level of knowledge. For this reason, he is considered 'the special bulwark and glory of the Catholic faith'.[143]

Furthermore, the encyclical highlights two additional aspects in which Aquinas is regarded as an unparalleled authority. These are the profound depths of his philosophical principles and the harmonious integration of faith and reason. He is presented as an exemplar of philosophical inquiry, investigating

---

[138] *AP,* n. 14. [139] *AP,* n. 16. [140] *AP,* n. 15. [141] *AP,* n. 16. [142] *AP,* n. 17.
[143] *AP,* n. 17.

the intrinsic nature of reality and principles through profound reflection, thereby mastering the discipline of philosophy in an exceptional manner. Furthermore, his philosophical expertise enabled him to excel in the field of apologetics. As evidenced in the Leonine document, 'he also used this philosophic method in the refutation of error, he won this title to distinction for himself: that, single-handed, he victoriously combated the errors of former times, and supplied invincible arms to put those to rout which might in after-times spring up'.[144] The hyperbolic language is evident: Aquinas is depicted as the indomitable champion of Christianity.

This tone, which may be characterised as absolutely triumphalist, is also maintained in order to describe the last element in which Aquinas shows himself to be unparalleled: the relationship between faith and reason. Indeed, he differentiates between these two domains while simultaneously integrating them in a virtuous circle. This enables faith to enlighten reason, and reason, illuminated by faith, to attain even more profound truths. From this profound union, the encyclical proceeds to state that reason, as elucidated by Aquinas, has reached its pinnacle of understanding: 'reason, borne on the wings of Thomas to its human height, can scarcely rise higher, while faith could scarcely expect more or stronger aids from reason than those which she has already obtained through Thomas'.[145]

In light of these words, it appears that philosophical and theological research has reached a point of completion. If, reason has reached its culmination with Aquinas, then both philosophical truths and truths of faith cannot be investigated in any greater depth than Aquinas has already done. It thus follows that the sole viable way for future inquiry is to maintain and reiterate the existing corpus of Aquinas' teachings.

This is why the final section of this historical digression is dedicated to demonstrating that throughout the centuries, Aquinas has consistently been embraced by all Catholic scholars and his teachings have invariably been regarded as the epitome of orthodoxy, to the extent that he has been bestowed with honours that have never been conferred upon any other Catholic theologian.[146]

In light of the aforementioned arguments, it becomes evident that there is a discernible ideological underpinning. The philosophers examined in this historical overview, from the church Fathers to the Scholastics, including Aquinas, are considered solely in their role as thinkers who adhered to the correct philosophical approach outlined in the encyclical's opening section. It is therefore evident that the goal of this presentation is not to provide a detailed or

---

[144] *AP*, n. 18.   [145] *AP*, n. 18.   [146] *AP*, n. 19–22.

exhaustive analysis of their philosophical ideas. Instead, it seeks to show that the Fathers and Scholastics, with Aquinas as the foremost figure, stand as the only models in philosophy truly deserving of emulation.

Furthermore, it is also crucial to highlight the reductionist approach that underlies these sections of the encyclical. Indeed, the primacy of Aquinas among these philosophers entails a reductionism of what is considered Christian philosophy to that of Aquinas' philosophy, which, in a certain sense, can and must be considered the epitome of all philosophy. If Aquinas represents the pinnacle of scholastic philosophy and the latter represents an exemplary synthesis of Christian philosophy, which is the only philosophic tradition that can be considered valid, then Aquinas can also be regarded as the definitive model for all philosophical thought.[147] Furthermore, if Aquinas represents the synthesis of all conceivable philosophies, there is no longer a need to turn to other philosophers, as his ideas are inherently sufficient for philosophical inquiry and the refutation of erroneous beliefs. Consequently, the encyclical paves the way for the emergence of a *maximalist Thomism*, which will rapidly disseminate throughout the Catholic world as a unified conceptual framework.

2.2.4 Part 3: False Philosophy and Remedies against It

In light of the fundamental principles that underpin the 'authentic philosophy', the encyclical continues to examine the characteristics of what might be called, by contrast, 'false philosophy'. This kind of philosophy, which has emerged in the modern times, represents a significant departure from the traditional pattern of thought that is rooted in faith and subject to the authority of revelation and the church, thus giving rise to a novel and potentially dangerous phenomenon.

> To the old teaching a novel system of philosophy has succeeded here and there, in which We fail to perceive those desirable and wholesome fruits which the Church and civil society itself would prefer. For it pleased the struggling innovators of the sixteenth century to philosophize without any respect for faith, the power of inventing in accordance with his own pleasure and bent being asked and given in turn by each one. Hence, it was natural that systems of philosophy multiplied beyond measure, and conclusions differing and clashing one with another arose about those matters even which are the most important in human knowledge. From a mass of conclusions men often come to wavering and doubt; and who knows not how easily the mind slips from doubt to error?[148]

---

[147] For an analysis of Thomism as the pinnacle of Christian philosophy see Piolanti, *Il tomismo*.
[148] *AP*, n. 24.

It is important to recognise that this philosophical approach is a product of modern thought, which emerged in the aftermath of the Protestant Reformation. The Reformation aimed to break the connection with authority and instead elevate the value of the individual's private judgment. As a result, it is possible to argue that the subject becomes the ultimate authority unto itself. In theology, this approach permits the free interpretation of Scripture and dogma, thereby eliminating the interpretive role once held by the church's magisterium. In philosophy, it fosters an interpretation of reality by human reason that is independent from faith and no longer constrained by external limitations. Consequently, it becomes clear that human reason, free from restrictions, assumes the role of the sole authority governing its own judgment.[149]

In light of these considerations, the encyclical reiterates the inherent dangers of this philosophical approach, which ultimately results in chaos and confusion, as demonstrated by the proliferation of diverse and conflicting doctrines. Consequently, this type of philosophy cannot be considered a viable means for understanding reality as conceived by God and cannot serve as the basis for sound philosophical reasoning. A philosophy that breeds doubt and fails to provide truth is, therefore, fundamentally flawed.

The encyclical proceeds to elucidate that this philosophical approach has also permeated the Catholic world, thereby endangering the integrity of divine doctrine.[150] The reference to the philosophical and theological pluralism that characterised Catholicism at least until the mid nineteenth century is evident. Consequently, the papal document reiterates the necessity to return to a single and unambiguous methodology in both philosophy and theology: a methodology, which binds together reason and revelation, 'may continue to be the invincible bulwark of faith'.[151] It thus appears that the sole means of countering the threat posed by erroneous modern philosophy is a return to the sound ancient doctrine, that of the Fathers and Scholastics.[152]

From these premises, it is evident that Aquinas' thought plays a pivotal role in this struggle. If the remedy for error is Scholasticism and if the invincible champion of the Scholasticism is Aquinas, it follows that he is the most powerful remedy against all forms of false philosophy.

> Domestic and civil society even, which, as all see, is exposed to great danger from this plague of perverse opinions, would certainly enjoy a far more peaceful and secure existence if a more wholesome doctrine were taught in the universities and high schools-one more in conformity with the teaching of the Church, such as is contained in the works of Thomas Aquinas. For, the teachings of Thomas on the true meaning of liberty, which at this time is

---

[149] *AP*, n. 27. [150] *AP*, n. 24. [151] *AP*, n. 24. [152] *AP*, n. 27.

running into license, on the divine origin of all authority, on laws and their force, on the paternal and just rule of princes, on obedience to the higher powers, on mutual charity one toward another – on all of these and kindred subjects – have very great and invincible force to overturn those principles of the new order which are well known to be dangerous to the peaceful order of things and to public safety.[153]

The doctrine of Aquinas is thus perceived as a compendium, or rather as a 'recipe book', from which to derive the appropriate antidote to counter any contemporary deviation. Furthermore, the encyclical's content reveals an unexpected connection between the recovery of Aquinas' philosophy and the restoration of a stable and just social order. It is crucial to note that the errors resulting from this modern philosophical approach extend beyond the domain of theoretical and speculative inquiry; such errors also have a tangible and impact on practical and social matters. Indeed, when erroneous philosophical principles are applied to society, it becomes evident that the entire social order will be undermined and rebuilt on different foundations. Accordingly, the encyclical asserts the necessity of reviving Aquinas' doctrine. It is only by recovering the teachings of Aquinas, who represents an unattainable exemplar in philosophical and theological doctrine, that society can be restored to its original sound principles, namely those willed by God.

In order to accomplish the project of philosophical renewal based on Thomism, the encyclical, in its concluding exhortation, outlines three practical ways of action, guided by three inspiring principles: universality, openness and authenticity.[154] Firstly, the necessity 'to restore the golden wisdom of St. Thomas and disseminate it widely for the defence and advancement of the Catholic faith, for the benefit of society and for the betterment of all sciences' is reiterated.[155] It is therefore recommended that new academic institutions should be established where only Thomistic philosophy and theology are taught, thus enabling young people to develop in accordance with Aquinas' orthodox doctrine. Finally, the encyclical calls for a renewed engagement with Aquinas' thought, drawing upon its original sources, in order to gain a deeper understanding of his teaching in its most authentic form.[156]

The results were prompt. In October 1879, approximately two months after the publication of *Aeterni Patris*, Pope Leo XIII established the Pontifical Academy of Saint Thomas Aquinas in Rome.[157] This marked the beginning of a series of similar institutions that, based on the programme outlined in *Aeterni Patris*, would proliferate throughout Europe in the following decades. Furthermore, in 1880, Leo XIII proceeded to establish the *Commissio Leonina*

---

[153] *AP,* n. 28–29.   [154] Perini, 'Dall' "Aeterni Patris"', 628–629.   [155] *AP,* n. 31.
[156] *AP,* n. 31.   [157] Leo XIII, *Iampridem considerando*.

(Leonine Commission) and ordered the preparation and publication of a critical edition of Aquinas' works.[158] Finally, on 4 August 1880, Aquinas was proclaimed Doctor of the church and patron of all Catholic schools and universities, thus sealing the Leonine philosophical reform. This process effectively marked the beginning of a new era in Catholic culture, where Thomism became the dominant doctrine.

2.3 The Social-Political Project of Leo XIII

In light of the investigation into the encyclical *Aeterni Patris*, it is now possible to observe the profound implications this document had on the Catholic culture of the time. As previously stated, the objective of *Aeterni Patris* was the revitalisation of Thomistic philosophy. Nevertheless, such an endeavour should not be confined to purely philosophical or strictly theological domains. The recovery of Thomism, as envisaged by Pope Leo XIII, is regarded as a vital instrument for combating the errors of modern society. These errors originate from a rationalist philosophy that glorifies the principle of autonomous reason, thereby undermining the principle of authority. Consequently, the resurgence of Thomism plays a pivotal role in the political and social realms, as it is conceived as an effective means of restoring society in accordance with Christian principles and in opposition to liberal and socialist ideologies.

From this perspective, the action of Leo XIII can be understood in continuity with those of his predecessor, Pius IX. Both popes were firmly opposed to modern society, thus aligning with the typical Catholic intransigence. However, while Pius IX was engaged in political conflict and was staunchly opposed to any form of liberal regime, openly condemning any form of conciliation with modern society, in contrast, Leo XIII shifted the confrontation to an intellectual and philosophical plane, abandoning the harsh tones of political conflict.

As De Rosa notes, the cessation of political contention and the resulting reduction in tensions do not indicate that Leo XIII adopted conciliatory attitudes, thereby initiating a dialogue with modern society. Conversely, despite modifying his stance, he remained firmly committed to his intransigence. Leo XIII was convinced that the optimal solution to the social ills was the creation of a single, uniform system of thought capable of addressing the challenges of modern society. In other words, the pontiff 'far from abandoning intransigence in Italy, aimed to transform it into a constructive, positive force, close to the people and responsive to their vital needs. It was thus necessary for clergy and

---

[158] Leo XIII, *Placere nobis*.

laity to study and improve their ability to respond positively to the liberal offensive with the help of the "sound Catholic philosophy"'.[159]

It is evident that the pontiff's idea of social restoration in accordance with Christian principles is based on the reestablishment of a robust Christian intellectual tradition, that is Thomism, to counter opposing doctrines. Consequently, any alternative approach to political and social reconstruction would have been futile and unfeasible without the imposition of a unified and rigorous philosophical discipline across all Catholic educational institutions globally. In summary, it is possible to observe that Leo XIII's promotion of Thomism was not just a philosophical initiative but also a political response. He believed that restoring the Christian social order was essential to addressing social problems and countering revolutionary threats. Like many other intransigent Catholics of his time, Leo XIII perceived Thomism as a defence against subversive ideologies that undermined traditional values in family, society, and politics.

The Thomistic concept of substantial unity provides Leo XIII with a conceptual framework that legitimises the church's political and social role. Accordingly, the church is conceived as the *substantial form* of society, in a manner analogous to the soul, which is regarded as the substantial form of the body. This analogy implies that the church is the principle that confers both form and life upon society as a whole. Consequently, the state is expected to be united with the church and subject to its spiritual authority. Such a configuration constitutes the ideal model for a just civil society that enables individuals to attain their proper ends.[160]

From this perspective, Thomism, understood as the only Christian philosophy and a unified foundational thought, becomes the useful and necessary tool to justify and re-propose the classical ecclesiological model based on the Bellarminian concept of the *potestas indirecta* (the indirect power in temporal matters), in which church and state are both called to form civil society, each acting in its own field and with its own means.[161] Nevertheless, in light of this idea, notable distinctions emerge between the church and the State, both regarded as *societates perfectae* (perfect societies), in terms of their intrinsic nature and fundamental purpose.[162] The church is a supernatural entity whose

---

[159] '[Leone XIII] lungi dall'abbandonare l'intransigenza in Italia, pensava di trasformarla, pensava di farne una forza costruttiva, positiva, vicino al popolo e sensibile alle sue vitali esigenze. Preti e laici dovevano studiare e aumentare le proprie capacità di rispondere positivamente all'offensiva liberale sulla base della "sana filosofia cattolica"'. De Rosa, 'Introduzione', 87.

[160] Leo XIII would develop this idea in the encyclical *Immortale Dei* in which the relationship between church and state and its function in guiding society is examined.

[161] On Bellarmine's doctrine of *potestas indirecta* see Tutino, *Empire of Souls*.

[162] On the philosophical-legal concept of *societas perfecta*, see Schrader, *De hominum societate generatim*.

aim is the attainment of the supernatural good of its members, whereas the state is a natural reality whose aim is the promotion of earthly wellbeing amongst its citizens.[163] Furthermore, since citizens of states, as Christians, are also members of the church, it follows that the church certainly has the right and duty to intervene directly in the lives of Christians in matters pertaining to spiritual salvation. At the same time, it also has the right and duty to intervene indirectly in those temporal matters that, although falling under the direct jurisdiction of states, somehow touch upon matters of faith and morals.[164] Therefore, since certain temporal issues are directly related to eternal salvation, they indirectly pertain to ecclesiastical jurisdiction. In these cases, the church is obliged to intervene with its teachings and actions, thereby exercising its influence. This approach demonstrates that, on the one hand, the church asserts its right to exercise direct jurisdiction over its subjects; on the other hand, it indirectly claims the task of influencing, or perhaps it would be more accurate to say, forming, civil society through its influence on consciences, since the subjects of both societies are the same.

This concept enabled Leo XIII to establish a position between a theocratic system that was no longer viable in modern society and the liberal thesis of a complete separation between church and state.[165] On the basis of Thomism and its theoretical principles, the pontiff seeks to re-establish the church's influence in an increasingly secularised world.[166]

Against this backdrop, it is evident that the Thomistic renewal desired by Pope Leo XIII represents not only the recovery of the sole genuine philosophy within the Catholic tradition, but also an indispensable instrument for achieving a comprehensive political and social reform. In other words, Thomism must be considered as a functional instrument for the formation of a renewed Christian worldview.

3 The Reception of the Encyclical *Aeterni Patris*: Two Different Interpretative Models

This study began by examining the gradual resurgence of Thomism at the dawn of the nineteenth century, situated within the context of intransigent Catholicism. Section 2 introduced Pope Leo XIII's encyclical *Aeterni Patris*, regarded as the definitive programmatic manifesto for the advancement of Thomistic philosophy within the Catholic framework.

Against this backdrop, the present section investigates the reception and implications of *Aeterni Patris*, with particular attention to the various

---

[163] *Immortale Dei*, n. 10–11. [164] *Immortale Dei*, n. 13. [165] *Immortale Dei*, n. 14–17.
[166] *Immortale Dei*, n. 29–33; Lamberts, 'Religious, Political', 33–34.

interpretations of the papal document. To this end, two authoritative contemporary commentaries are presented and compared: Giovanni Maria Cornoldi's *La regola filosofica di Sua Santità Leone P.P. XIII proposta nell'enciclica Aeterni Patris*,[167] and Carlo Passaglia's *Sulla dottrina di San Tommaso secondo l'enciclica di Leone XIII*. Among the many studies on *Aeterni Patris*, these two have been selected for two principal reasons: Cornoldi's work constitutes the first comprehensive and officially endorsed analysis of the encyclical, while Passaglia's monograph offers a direct critical response to Cornoldi's interpretation. This comparison, therefore, provides valuable insight into the contemporary Catholic intellectual climate and the earliest interpretations of the Thomistic revival promoted by the encyclical.

3.1 The 'Essential' Thomism of Giovanni Maria Cornoldi

From September to November 1879, a mere month after the publication of *Aeterni Patris*, a comprehensive commentary on the Leonine encyclical was published in the pages of *La Civiltà Cattolica*. This commentary was authored by Cornoldi. Malusa, the most authoritative scholar on the Venetian Jesuit, asserts that this commentary was not only the most timely on the papal document, but can also be considered the official interpretation of the document, given that it was written for *La Civiltà Cattolica*, that is, the Jesuit journal which can be considered the semi-official voice of the Holy See.[168]

Cornoldi was a fervent Thomist whose work was entirely aimed at reviving the thought of Aquinas according to the maximalist and ideological vision typical of the Jesuit environment of *La Civiltà Cattolica*.[169] He perceived the Leonine encyclical as a confirmation of the philosophical tenets he had been espousing over time. This last aspect establishes a kind of circularity between Cornoldi's Thomistic maximalism and the philosophical reductionism of *Aeterni Patris*, whereby each reinforces the other. The Leonine document appears to be clearly influenced by the Thomistic vision of the intransigent Jesuit circles, and at the same time, this conception draws new strength from the authority of the document itself.[170] Consequently, Cornoldi's interpretation of *Aeterni Patris* can be seen as an attempt to justify and disseminate his maximalist positions by leveraging the force and authority of the papal document.

---

[167] In 1880, this text was published under the title *La riforma della filosofia promossa dall'enciclica Aeterni Patris di S.S. Leone XIII*. Henceforth, the 1880 text will be quoted, as it is identical in all respects to the 1879 edition of *La Civiltà Cattolica*.
[168] Malusa, *Neotomismo*, vol. 1, 262–226.
[169] For an analysis of Cornoldi's philosophical thought and his battles in favour of Thomism, see Malusa, *Neotomismo*, vol. 1, 1–248.
[170] Malusa, *Neotomismo*, vol. 1, 263.

Cornoldi's commentary is divided into three lengthy chapters, which more or less follow the themes explored in *Aeterni Patris*. Chapter 1 presents an analysis of the first part of the encyclical, wherein Cornoldi outlines the foundational elements of what he terms *la Regola Filosofica* (The Philosophical Rule). In this section, the Jesuit offers an account of the essential attributes of sound philosophy.[171] Chapter 2 is devoted to investigating *la Regola Filosofica considerata in sé stessa* (the Philosophical Rule considered in itself), which constitutes the core of the Leonine philosophical reform, according to Cornoldi's interpretation. In this chapter, the author presents and summarises the fundamental principles of Thomism in a clear and unambiguous manner, providing a sort of comprehensive compendium of the key tenets of this philosophical tradition.[172] Finally, Chapter 3 examines the implications of this philosophical stance.[173] Here, Cornoldi addresses two distinct groups: those who openly rebel against this approach, referred to as the heterodox,[174] and those who are orthodox and comply with the papal directives.[175] Within this framework, the Venetian Jesuit identifies a considerable number of Catholics who, despite outwardly demonstrating obedience, interpret the teachings of the encyclical in a diametrically opposed way to the genuine intentions of the pontiff.[176] The concluding paragraph of Chapter 3 is devoted to an examination of the practical implementation of the Philosophical Rule, offering insights into the measures desired by Leo XIII for the widespread dissemination of Thomism within the Catholic community.[177]

3.1.1 The Dogmatic Character of the Thomism

Cornoldi's text is clearly apologetic. This aspect is evident from the outset, as evidenced by the use of militaristic language. In the text, Leo XIII is portrayed as a military leader who, in the conflict between truth and error, gathers an army to lead a crusade against those who oppose true philosophy. The weapon in the pontiff's hand is the encyclical *Aeterni Patris*, which establishes the philosophical rule to be universally followed within the Catholic world.[178] Catholics are thus urged to unite under the pontiff's directives, avoiding the dispersion of their efforts by pursuing false philosophies, which Cornoldi equates to 'vain dreams'.[179]

Cornoldi then proceeds to examine the nature of true philosophy, listing eight essential features derived from the encyclical *Aeterni Patris*.[180] This description emphasises a philosophy that is wholly supportive of and aligned with the tenets

---

[171] Cornoldi, *La riforma*, 27–46. [172] Cornoldi, *La riforma*, 46–71.
[173] Cornoldi, *La riforma*, 71–151. [174] Cornoldi, *La riforma*, 71–96.
[175] Cornoldi, *La riforma*, 96–97, 121–125. [176] Cornoldi, *La riforma*, 98–121.
[177] Cornoldi, *La riforma*, 126–151. [178] Cornoldi, *La riforma*, 25–27.
[179] 'Sogni vani'. Cornoldi, *La riforma*, 29. [180] Cornoldi, *La riforma*, 31–35.

of faith and revelation. Philosophical reason finds its origin and ultimate fulfilment in faith. The objective of philosophical inquiry is to elucidate the natural truths that provide the foundation for faith. However, despite being natural, these truths are inherent to God, who is the ultimate truth, and thus, explicitly or implicitly, form part of the deposit of faith.[181] Consequently, while philosophy is responsible for demonstrating natural truths within a philosophical and rational framework, it does not act autonomously but is situated within a broader context, preceded by faith, where even these natural truths find their origin.[182] According to Cornoldi, the strength and dignity of reason and philosophical inquiry arise from faith. By incorporating philosophy, the *depositum fidei* is enhanced and developed. Consequently, philosophy assumes a dogmatic character, being indissolubly linked to faith and divine revelation.

Cornoldi elucidates the close connection between philosophy and faith through the Thomistic theory of the substantial unity between soul and body:

> The relationship between faith and philosophy is very close: I would compare it to that of the soul with the human body. The human body provides immense services to the soul, and indeed the soul depends on it for the beginning of its existence. In the same way, faith must regard philosophy as its faithful handmaid, since it derives great benefit from reason: and although faith is nobler than reason, which is the source of philosophy, just as the soul is nobler than the body, nevertheless the former cannot exist except in a rational subject, and thus associated with reason itself.[183]

This analogy has significant implications for Cornoldian reasoning on the relationship between faith and reason. On the one hand, it serves to reinforce the ancillary nature of philosophy in relation to faith, namely, the idea that philosophy must support and reinforce faith. On the other hand, it suggests a structural dependence of philosophy on faith. By further developing the soul–body analogy, it is possible to observe that the body, in itself, is devoid of existence unless it is animated by the soul. Thus, if this analogy is applied to the reason–faith relationship, it becomes clear that reason, in itself, lacks the capacity for self-actualization unless it is animated by faith. In other words, faith enables reason to achieve its full potential. Consequently, echoing Malusa who makes clear Cornoldi's reasoning, it is possible to state that reason 'does not exist prior to faith, but if it exists, it exists only as a set of elements that

---

[181] Cornoldi, *La riforma*, 31.   [182] Malusa, *Neotomismo*, vol. 1, 266.
[183] 'Il nesso tra le fede e la filosofia è strettissimo: lo dirò simile a quello dell'anima col corpo umano. Il corpo umano presta all'anima immensi servigi, anzi questa ne dipende per esordire la propria esistenza. Egualmente la fede dee riguardare la filosofia come sua fida ancella, onde trae utilità immensa: e comeché la fede sia più nobile della ragione ch'è fonte della filosofia, come l'anima è più nobile del corpo; tuttavia quella non può esistere che in un soggetto ragionevole e quindi associata alla ragione medesima'. Cornoldi, *La riforma*, 36.

become real when they receive the form of faith'.[184] Paraphrasing the Thomistic principle of the substantial unity, faith can be regarded as the substantial form of reason. From this perspective, philosophy, as an expression of reason, is devoid of any inherent connotation when considered in itself, namely, before its unification with faith. This is analogous to the body's lack of capacity for self-actualisation prior to its union with the soul. On the contrary, when philosophy is informed by faith and thus aims at truth, it acquires the character of Christian philosophy. On the basis of Cornoldi's assumptions, philosophy can only be classified as either false, that is, a philosophy that tends towards falsehood and error, or as Christian philosophy.

The Jesuit proceeds to demonstrate how the church Fathers and Scholastics consistently affirmed the capacity of reason to give rise to an authentic Christian philosophy. These Christian philosophers and theologians never deviated from these principles. Despite utilising the works of ancient pagan philosophers, they consistently reinterpreted them in the context of faith and divine revelation.[185] This approach to philosophy thus serves as a tangible manifestation of the aforementioned model, wherein faith represents the ultimate criterion for evaluating the soundness of philosophical reasoning, as it encompasses the truths that reason is tasked with investigating. Faith, asserts Cornoldi, 'being truth, is by nature incompatible with error; however, it would be unwise to establish a false philosophy as its handmaid'.[186]

According to Cornoldi, Aquinas epitomises this philosophical approach, as he defines and organises the principles of Christian philosophy in a way that ensures such a philosophy is an integral part of the life of the church. Aquinas' doctrine thus represents the most reliable and unparalleled model of Christian philosophy, given that his philosophical theories, especially the doctrine of substantial unity, have consistently been endorsed by the magisterium of the church.[187]

This approach has twofold implications: firstly, the reductionism of philosophy to Thomism and secondly, the dogmatisation of Thomism itself. If philosophy can only be Christian philosophy, and if Thomism is the model of this philosophy, then Thomism can be regarded as the only expression of the true philosophy. Furthermore, since Aquinas' philosophical theories have consistently received papal approval, they must be considered as true doctrines of the faith, thereby acquiring a dogmatic character. From this perspective, Cornoldi's

---

[184] '[La ragione] non ha esistenza anteriormente alla fede, ma ... se esiste, esiste solo come insieme di elementi che divengono una realtà all'atto del ricevere la forma della fede'. Malusa, *Neotomismo*, vol. 1, 267–268.

[185] Cornoldi, *La riforma*, 37.

[186] '[La fede] essendo verità, ... è per sua natura inconciliabile con l'errore; però stolta cosa sarebbe stata stabilirne in qualità di ancella una falsa filosofia'. Cornoldi, *La riforma*, 37.

[187] Cornoldi, *La riforma*, 38.

maximalism becomes evident, elevating Aquinas to the status of unquestioned authority in the Catholic world.

Furthermore, if Thomism is considered the definitive philosophical doctrine, the rejection of such a system would inevitably result in a state of uncertainty and potential errors in philosophical inquiry. Cornoldi attributes the errors of modern philosophy to the gradual rejection of Thomistic doctrines. The loss of the principle of substantial unity between reason and faith, and the subsequent separation of reason from faith, results in the emergence of a self-referential and self-authoritative form of philosophy.[188] This philosophical aberration is evidenced by the transition from a Thomistic worldview, which espouses a harmonious and unified understanding of reality, to a Protestant Reformation-influenced worldview characterised by disintegration and subjectivity.[189] The result is the fragmentation of thought, leading to a philosophical pluralism that only creates instability and insecurity, even affecting the Catholic world.

> On the one hand, according to Cornoldi, there is a mad and impious philosophy that corrupts everything and, from the destruction of the speculative order, rushes to the destruction of the practical order; on the other hand, there is constant fluctuation and instability, so that Catholics, divided and doubtful, are not well equipped to combat error and prevent the infinite evils that befall the Church and civil society.[190]

The only remedy for such a decline is the reform of philosophy as proposed in *Aeterni Patris*. This entails the implementation of a philosophical renewal based on the recovery and restoration of Thomistic thought as the sole philosophical model for the Catholic world.[191] Cornoldi's maximalist interpretation of Thomism is once again evident. For the Venetian Jesuit, Aquinas' philosophy represents the only complete philosophical system. It is a philosophy so true that it can and must be reconciled and integrated with modern scientific theories, and can demonstrate the real inconsistency and falsity of all the other opposing systems.[192] Consequently, the logical conclusion of Cornoldian maximalism is the denial of freedom of thought in the philosophical realm. Such freedom leads to the rejection of a common philosophical system, namely that of Thomistic philosophy, and perpetuates the very individualism that causes all philosophical disorders.[193]

---

[188] Cornoldi, *La riforma*, 41.   [189] Cornoldi, *La riforma*, 40.
[190] 'Da una parte abbiamo una filosofia pazza ed empia che tutto corrompe e dalla distruzione dell'ordine speculativo corre alla distruzione dell'ordine pratico; dall'altra parte abbiamo una continua fluttuazione ed instabilità, per la quale i cattolici, divisi tra loro e dubbiosi, sono poco acconci a debellare l'errore ed impedire mali infiniti che sopravvengono alla Chiesa ed alla civile società'. Cornoldi, *La riforma*, 42.
[191] Cornoldi, *La riforma*, 50.   [192] Cornoldi, *La riforma*, 43–44.
[193] Cornoldi, *La riforma*, 52.

3.1.2 The Philosophical Rule

Against this backdrop, Cornoldi presents what he terms the Philosophical Rule of Leo XIII,[194] which encompasses the practical principles articulated by the Pope in *Aeterni Patris*.[195] These principles, according to Cornoldi, should serve as the foundation for reforming Catholic philosophy and as a guiding principle for all Catholics. As Malusa points out,

> The novelty of the encyclical is considerable: it explicitly forbids any philosopher who claims to be Christian from engaging in philosophy in the manner of a non-Christian. Moreover, it condemns approaches rooted in anti-Catholic or erroneous philosophies. For a true believer, philosophy must be grounded in Thomistic principles, as these are the only ones that harmonize philosophy with Christian doctrine.[196]

According to Cornoldi the first rule in implementing the philosophical reform is to re-establish a sound and error-free philosophy. This approach ensures that those engaged in philosophical inquiry can avoid to be entangled in lengthy and inconclusive speculative debates, which could otherwise lead to erroneous and potentially dangerous conclusions. Consequently, their arguments must be grounded in truths that are already established as certain and reliable. This sound philosophy is, of course, the Christian philosophy that Thomism fully and perfectly expresses.[197] The consequence of this approach is the explicit rejection of any form of philosophical eclecticism: namely, an approach that relies on individual reason and the analysis of various philosophical systems to identify truth, often resulting in an inquisitive and speculative philosophy.[198] Therefore, according to Cornoldi, as any form of inquisitive inquiry based on individual reason is rejected, it follows that philosophy must be founded on the principle of authority. Only with an authoritative model as its foundation can philosophy develop and progress towards deeper understanding.[199] Within this framework, Thomism emerges as the authoritative and indispensable model to be promoted in all Catholic schools, providing the foundation for any secure philosophical inquiry capable of genuine scientific progress. However, such progress is necessarily circumscribed by the intrinsic limits of philosophy. Philosophy embraces both theoretical and practical reasoning, yet it remains bounded by two frontiers: first, the 'experimental cognition of singulars,' that is,

---

[194] Cornoldi, *La riforma*, 53–54. [195] *AP*, n. 31.
[196] 'La novità dell'enciclica è forte: si vieta al filosofo che si professa cristiano di filosofare alla stregua di chi cristiano non è e si vietano tutti gli approcci alle filosofie anticattoliche ed erronee. Filosofare per un credente significa accettare i principi tomistici, i soli che accordano la filosofia al cristianesimo'. Malusa, *Neotomismo*, vol. 1, 273.
[197] Cornoldi, *La riforma*, 55–56. [198] Cornoldi, *La riforma*, 54–55.
[199] Cornoldi, *La riforma*, 56–57.

the domain of concrete empirical experience; and second, the 'cognition of the supra-intelligible,' that is, the realm of Christian dogmas.[200] These constitute the inherent limits of philosophy, for the former cannot yield scientific knowledge of essential principles—since it merely describes particular phenomena without disclosing their causes or universal essences—while the latter surpasses the capacities of natural reason. Human reason can only perceive the limits of these supra-intelligible realities or apprehend them in partial aspects; it cannot establish evident propositions concerning the subject–predicate connection they entail. Consequently, according to Cornoldi, everything that falls within these two boundaries constitutes the proper object of philosophy and occupies a clearly delimited place within the context of Aquinas's thought.

Furthermore, the Philosophical Rule is required to address the specific methodologies by which philosophy should be taught in Catholic institutions. Given that the teaching of Aquinas is regarded as the paradigm of philosophical thought, it can be deduced that the teaching of philosophy must adhere to Thomistic principles. Consequently, in this second part of his commentary, Cornoldi focuses on delineating the persons involved in and the instruments necessary for the widespread dissemination of Thomism.

The main actors in this initiative are bishops and professors of philosophy. In the first place, the responsibility for implementing the programme of philosophical reform desired by the Pope falls to the Bishops, to whom the encyclical is addressed and who have the direct government of all the faithful. In practice, their duty is to disseminate the principles of Thomistic philosophy and to ensure that Thomism is taught in an accurate and appropriate manner.[201] Consequently, in order to fulfil this obligation, they are also responsible for the selection of the teachers who will be assigned to the seminaries and other Catholic educational institutions. It is therefore incumbent upon professors, who represent the second essential actor for the realisation of the philosophical reform, to be of unquestionable Thomistic faith. In this context, the professors chosen by the bishops are not granted the same freedom in philosophical teaching as other lay people. Indeed, they are subordinated to ecclesiastical jurisdiction in their teaching and are expected to faithfully echo the official voice of the church, with the aim of convincing and persuading their students that Aquinas' doctrine is superior to all others. Those who do not adhere to these principles and instead propagate other philosophical theories are obliged to resign from their teaching roles.[202] Through Cornoldi's maximalist interpretation, the unity of purpose with the ideas presented in *Aeterni Patris* – essential element for the realisation of

---

[200] 'Lo esperimentale dei singolari [e …] la cognizione del sopraintelligibile'. Cornoldi, *La riforma*, 62–63.
[201] Cornoldi, *La riforma*, 59–60.   [202] Cornoldi, *La riforma*, 61–62.

philosophical reform – is reshaped into a rigid and exclusive uniformity, leaving no space for any thought that diverges from or stands in opposition to Thomism.

To put the philosophical reform into practice, the Venetian Jesuit identified two fundamental instruments: the creation of academies and the implementation of philosophical classes. First of all, he praised Leo XIII's directive to create Thomistic academies of a universal and cosmopolitan character. These academies would facilitate the collaboration of eminent scholars from different backgrounds, including ecclesiastical and lay people, as well as professors of theology and philosophy, medicine, and the natural sciences. The goal of these institutions is twofold: firstly, they aim at deepening the study of Aquinas' philosophy and secondly, at demonstrating the possible unity of science and faith by means of Thomism.[203] Consequently, through their research programmes, these centres should function as real centres for disseminating Thomism.

Then, Cornoldi emphasises the necessity for philosophical classes to align with the tenets of Aquinas' genuine thought. In this way, they can be regarded as those 'pure streams', as described in *Aeterni Patris*, that derive directly from the source of Aquinas and maintain their clarity intact.[204] However, in order to advance the authentic Thomistic thought, it is first necessary to establish with certainty what the true Thomistic doctrine is. Consequently, applying the criterion of 'the certain and concordant judgment concerning the interpretation of the Angelic doctrine', Cornoldi outlines eleven simple axioms that define the fundamental principles of Thomism.[205] The eleven principles are as follows: (1) The substantial and accidental reality of corporeal things; (2) Substantial and accidental change; (3) Prime matter distinct from substantial form; (4) Real distinction between accidents and substance; (5) There is a single substantial form in human beings, and it is the intellectual soul; (6) The intellectual soul is the only subsistent, immaterial, incorruptible, and immortal substantial form; (7) The intellectual soul is not generated by human being but is created by God; (8) The intellectual cognition of the intellectual soul occurs through the agent intellect; (9) All intelligible species derive from the abstraction performed by the intellect; (10) God is the source of both faith and reason, so there can be no contradiction between faith and reason; and (11) Distinction between uncreated and created being; each thing has its own being that is separate from the being of other things.[206]

This compendium presents an interpretative grid for determining the consistency of various interpretations of Aquinas' thought with the genuine Thomistic doctrine. It thus enables the ascertainment of whether these interpretations can

---

[203] Cornoldi, *La riforma*, 64–66. [204] Cornoldi, *La riforma*, 66. See also *AP*, n. 31.

[205] '*La certa e concorde sentenza* intorno alla spiegazione della dottrina dell'Angelico'. Cornoldi, *La riforma*, 67.

[206] Cornoldi, *La riforma*, 67–68.

be classified as 'pure streams' of Thomism and therefore disseminated, or whether they should be prohibited as 'impure streams'.[207]

Although Cornoldi is aware of the non-exhaustiveness of this schema, through this hermeneutical reductionism, he inaugurates a kind of Thomism that could be defined as 'essential'. This new approach aims at distilling Aquinas' doctrine into a set of fundamental principles that encapsulate its essence. This operation allows Cornoldi to achieve two different objectives. On the one hand, he precludes the possibility of any free interpretation that falls outside this predetermined framework.[208] On the other hand, he creates a powerful instrument for monitoring the evolution of Catholic philosophical thought.

The culmination of Cornoldi's 'essential' Thomism is exemplified in the publication of the twenty-four Thomistic theses, formulated by the Jesuit Guido Mattiussi (1852–1925). Mattiussi's theses, published in *La Civiltà Cattolica* between 1914 and 1916, were endorsed by the Sacred Congregation for Studies and were employed as a means of monitoring and censuring various modernist tendencies.[209] This constrained and ideologically driven interpretation of Aquinas leaves Catholics with the sole option of unquestioning obedience to this philosophical rule.[210]

The Cornoldian approach finds its immediate application in the latter part of his commentary, where the author analyses the behaviour of those who outwardly profess obedience to the philosophical rule of Pope Leo XIII. In light of the aforementioned background and the principles on which these believers base their pretended obedience, Cornoldi's Thomistic maximalism becomes particularly evident. Cornoldi summarises in seven propositions the attitudes of those who falsely obey the Leonine philosophical reform: (1) Pope Leo did not definitively dogmatise any of Aquinas' propositions, thus allowing for the teaching of any philosophy freely. (2) In light of the Pope's general advocacy of following Aquinas' doctrine without specifying which tenets should be followed and which should be eschewed, it is necessary to apply the famous patristic motto in *necessariis unitas sed in dubiis libertas*. (3) Pope Leo espouses an eclectic philosophy, which entails the acceptance of any wisdom conveyed by any individual. (4) In light of the Pope's teachings against disseminating falsehoods, it can be inferred that Aquinas' ideas, which have been disproven by scientific advancements, should not be taken into account. (5) The Pope's intention is to propose a genuine Christian philosophy; therefore, it is essential to exclude Aristotle's influence from Aquinas' teachings, retaining only the elements derived from the church Fathers. (6) Regarding the interpretation of Aquinas,

---

[207] Cornoldi, *La riforma*, 67.   [208] Cornoldi, *La riforma*, 68–69.
[209] Malusa, *Neotomismo*, vol. 2, 66–67; Mattiussi, *Le XXIV tesi*.
[210] Cornoldi, *La riforma*, 69.

the Pope does not stipulate a specific approach, thus allowing for the free interpretation of Thomism. (7) The syllogistic method of Scholasticism represents the optimal philosophical methodology. Consequently, it is sufficient to utilise this method, given that the strength of Scholastic philosophy resides in this method.[211]

According to the Venetian Jesuit, there can be no doubt about the dogmatic value of the philosophical rule. Consequently, Thomism, when correctly reinterpreted in the light of its fundamental principles, must be considered the only philosophy to be taught and disseminated in the Catholic world.

> If the Pope wants to introduce a *reform*, it is clear this doctrine was not taught previously, and now he wants it to be taught not only elsewhere, but also in Rome. ... It can be conceded that before the encyclical, there was a certain freedom in teaching Aquinas's philosophy, but it must be admitted that now the Pope does not leave the same freedom as before, otherwise, his orders and actions would be inexplicable.[212]

It is only through the implementation of a unified educational system that instills knowledge based on the principles of Thomism that the detrimental effects of modern philosophical ideologies can be mitigated and society can be protected from their adverse influence.[213] This is the ultimate objective of maximalist Thomism.

In conclusion, it can be asserted that Cornoldi's 'essential' Thomism, due to the drastic reductionism to which it subjects Aquinas' thought, does not present itself as a true, articulated, and complex philosophical system. It may therefore be regarded as a tool for controlling the entire Catholic philosophical landscape. Consequently, adherence to such a Thomism is not primarily concerned with an in-depth exploration of Aquinas' thought through direct analysis of his works. Rather, it signifies being faithful to specific doctrinal tenets which, although presented as the 'pure streams' of Aquinas' teaching, are in fact the product of an often indirect, selective, and apologetic interpretation of certain aspects of his philosophy. Therefore, the concept of maximalist Thomism, which is regarded as the sole viable philosophical model, can be seen as the result of a minimalist and reductionist approach to Aquinas' thought. It can be concluded that maximalist Thomism represents an ideological endeavour to crystallise and

---

[211] Cornoldi, *La riforma*, 98–102.

[212] 'Se il papa vuole introdotta una *riforma*, è chiaro che prima non si insegnava quella dottrina che ora vuole che venga insegnata non solo altrove, ma anche in Roma. ... Si conceda che prima dell'Enciclica vi sia stata una tal quale libertà d'insegnamento rispetto alla filosofia dell'Aquinate: ma insieme si dovrà ammettere che ora il Papa non lascia la medesima libertà che prima vi era: altrimenti sarebbe inesplicabile ciò ch' egli ordinò e fece'. Cornoldi, *La riforma*, 124–125.

[213] Cornoldi, *La riforma*, 128–129.

dogmatise certain principles derived from Aquinas. This is done with the objective of eliminating pluralism in order to combat the various errors of modern society in a uniform and coherent way.

3.2 The Philosophical Eclecticism of Carlo Passaglia

In 1880, Carlo Passaglia published his commentary on the encyclical *Aeterni Patris*. This work, which had previously been published in the journal *L'ateneo Religioso* as a series of short articles, is fully embedded in the lively debate on the interpretation of Leo XIII's document that animated the Catholic world at that time.[214]

Passaglia's objective in publishing this commentary was not merely to provide an analysis of *Aeterni Patris*. Rather, through a comprehensive examination of the text, he sought to challenge the prevailing maximalist tendencies that absolutised Thomism as the exclusive philosophical and theological system within the Catholic world. This work can therefore be classified as one of Passaglia's polemical works. However, in comparison to the vehement polemics that characterised Passaglia's writings of the 1860s, the tone here is more measured.[215] The former Jesuit does not directly assail the encyclical or the Pope. Nevertheless, Passaglia's commentary indirectly criticises Leo XIII's attempt to consider Thomism as the model of Christian philosophy. By openly questioning the hermeneutical maximalism of those he refers to as *'gli eccessivi'* (the maximalists) and by pointing out the potential dangers of such an approach, Passaglia more or less covertly reveals the weakness of the encyclical: namely, the reductionism of Christian philosophy to Thomism. If, as previously indicated, there is a sort of circularity between the maximalist interpretation and the philosophical reductionism of the encyclical, whereby these positions reinforce each other, it follows that challenging maximalism also entails criticising the philosophical reductionism that underpins it. In other words, Passaglia's entire project is an intelligent attempt to dismantle the encyclical, starting from the text of the encyclical itself.

---

[214] See Traniello, *Cattolicesimo conciliatorista*, 310, ft. 9. In light of the concise nature of the articles about two pages (according to Traniello's report), it seems reasonable to conclude that they represent Passaglia's initial approach to this question. It can therefore be hypothesised that Passaglia's work *Sulla dottrina di San Tommaso secondo l'enciclica di Leone XIII* is the fruit of the re-elaboration of these articles and not that these articles constitute Passaglia's monograph *tout court*. However, as the articles in question were not available for direct consultation, this hypothesis remains to be verified.

[215] The writings of Passaglia from the 1860s are characterised by a vehement critique of the Pope and the entire ecclesiastical establishment on matters pertaining to the delicate relationship between the church and the State, national unity and the temporal power of the church. These positions ultimately resulted in his excommunication and suspension *a divinis*: see Rossi, 'Carlo Passaglia', 579–595.

Passaglia's commentary is divided into thirty-nine paragraphs, plus a final appendix on the Rosminian question.[216] In this section, the author directs his attention to the complex topic of freedom of thought and its relationship to the advancement of philosophical and theological research. These aspects are jeopardised by the maximalist Thomism that gained strength in the wake of *Aeterni Patris*. Right from the preface, Passaglia expresses his reservations about the encyclical and its impact on Catholicism. These concerns stem from the fact that the Leonine document, by focusing on the revival of Aquinas' doctrine, gives rise to various and erroneous interpretations that, in fact, deviate from a correct understanding of *Aeterni Patris* itself.[217] Before offering an in-depth analysis of the papal document, Passaglia divides the various hermeneutical approaches into three groups. Echoing the ecclesiastical motto *in necessariis unitas, in dubiis libertas, in omnibus caritas*, he asserts that the sole approach to comprehending the intrinsic significance of the encyclical – which has to be situated within the context of the debatable questions, since it does not pertain to matters of faith – is to preserve the freedom of thought and interpretation.[218] Only in this way it will possible to carry out a free inquiry, which, far from being apologetic and ideological, will reveal the correct interpretation of *Aeterni Patris*.

Passaglia's commentary is structured around three main themes which correspond to the different sections of *Aeterni Patris*. The first, which is dedicated to the paragraphs of the encyclical in which Aquinas is presented as the definitive model of Christian philosophy,[219] is focused on the figure of Aquinas and the correct way to understand his philosophy. The second, which is centred on the initial paragraphs of the third part of *Aeterni Patris*,[220] provides a detailed examination of the concept of perennial philosophy. Finally, the third addresses what Cornoldi had defined as 'the Philosophical Rule of Leo XIII',[221] namely the practical means of spreading Thomism;[222] here Passaglia's stance on Thomism is made clear.

3.2.1 The Limits of Aquinas' Philosophy and Its Correspondence with Perennial Philosophy

Although Aquinas is considered a master, his figure cannot be absolutised.[223] As Passaglia notes, while Aquinas' work is undoubtedly significant and valuable, it shares similarities with that of other scholastic doctors and is not

---

[216] In the Appendix, Passaglia defended Rosminian positions and denounced the dangers inherent in maximalist Thomism. See Passaglia, *Sulla dottrina*, 309–363.
[217] Passaglia, *Sulla dottrina*, 4–5.   [218] Passaglia, *Sulla dottrina*, 4.   [219] *AP*, n. 17–23.
[220] *AP*, n. 24.   [221] Cornoldi, *La riforma*, 53–54.   [222] *AP*, n. 31.
[223] Passaglia, *Sulla dottrina*, 17–18.

immune to errors and limitations. It is necessary to situate the Angelic Doctor within the context of typical philosophical eclecticism that has characterised Christian schools since the time of the Fathers of the church.[224] Thus, like other Christian masters, Aquinas does not develop an original philosophical system of his own, but rather elaborates a complex and articulated doctrine rooted in the authentic Christian tradition.[225]

In the light of this initial observation, it is evident that Passaglia, by acknowledging the greatness of Aquinas in his eclecticism and integration into the Christian tradition, aims at challenging the maximalist interpretation that exalts Aquinas as the synthesis of all philosophy, thereby placing him above the entire tradition.

The former Jesuit proceeds to elucidate the limitations of the philosophy of the *Doctor Angelicus* through a historical rather than an ideological approach.[226] Although *Aeterni Patris* considers Aquinas' doctrine to be the most perfect, as 'philosophy has no part which he did not touch finely at once and thoroughly',[227] this does not imply that such a system should not be regarded as imperfect and limited. Indeed, if this were not the case, it would call into question the very nature of any philosophical system, which, as an expression of human reason, is always capable of being improved.[228] Therefore, Aquinas cannot be considered as the definitive authority in the field of philosophy.[229]

According to Passaglia, Aquinas' thought and philosophy must be considered in relation to the knowledge of that time. Therefore, if it can be stated with the encyclical's own words that Aquinas addressed every part of philosophy, this should be understood as limited to the philosophy of the thirteenth century and not to philosophy in general.[230] Thus, the attempt of those who seek in Aquinas' teaching clear and certain answers to the problems of contemporary society by reducing it to a sort of *ipse dixit* appears futile.

Furthermore, Passaglia stresses that, in order to fully comprehend the intrinsic value of Aquinas' teachings without falling into an unjustified apologetic defence, it is essential to consider how he develops his analysis. Therefore, in analysing the paragraph of the encyclical in which it is stated that Aquinas, through his clear and unambiguous methodology, has exhibited an unparalleled degree of expertise across a multitude of disciplines,[231] Passaglia effectively demonstrates that Aquinas reaches indisputable conclusions only in a very few cases, predominantly pertaining to the articles of Christian faith.[232] Conversely,

---

[224] Passaglia, *Sulla dottrina*, 14.   [225] Passaglia, *Sulla dottrina*, 232–258.
[226] Passaglia, *Sulla dottrina*, 18–19.   [227] *AP,* n. 17.   [228] Passaglia, *Sulla dottrina*, 24.
[229] Passaglia, *Sulla dottrina*, 37.   [230] Passaglia, *Sulla dottrina*, 20, 219–220.   [231] *AP,* n. 17.
[232] Passaglia, *Sulla dottrina*, 21.

the vast majority of his conclusions pertain to the domain of debatable opinions.[233]

> It follows that it is not possible to disagree with the motto *in dubiis libertas*, nor to wipe out *the difference* of assent that exists between *evident* theorems and *obscure* problems, or between *unchanging* science and *uncertain* opinions, which, though old and established, seem *probable* at one time and *false* at another. This is true not only of *physical and experimental* subjects, but also of *ideological, anthropological, cosmological, moral and legal* questions.[234]

The aforementioned limitations of Aquinas' system are particularly evident in the dialectic, the treatises on God, on incorporeal matters, and on human beings. These limits are also more evident in questions concerning perceptible things, such as cosmology, where the progress of scientific research cannot be ignored. Therefore, since Aquinas' thought appears limited in its arguments and conclusions, it follows that it can and should be further explored, discussed, and, if necessary, rejected. Furthermore, Passaglia continues, this last aspect is also evident in the history of the reception of Aquinas' thought, where his doctrine was never absolutised or considered free from errors.[235]

An additional notable constraint on Aquinas' philosophical perspective derives from Scholasticism itself. As Passaglia observed, the Scholastic period was deficient in the hermeneutical and critical tools that are essential for accurate philosophical and theological investigation.[236] The sources used were frequently unreliable, and there was a dearth of in-depth knowledge of the Greek language, which is an indispensable element for a direct engagement with the texts of the ancient philosophers and the church Fathers of the East. In the field of scholastic philosophy, Passaglia identifies the considerable impact of Aristotelian thought, which in turn was undermined by the use of semi-barbarous translations. Consequently, he suggests that it would be more appropriate to speak of '*Aristotelian philosophy* as expounded and annotated by the Scholastics' than of proper Scholastic philosophy.[237] In the field of philosophy, therefore, Aquinas should be regarded as a significant commentator and

---

[233] Passaglia, *Sulla dottrina*, 22.
[234] 'Arroge non potersi repugnare alla massima, *in dubiis libertas*; né potersi cancellare *la differenza* dell'assenso, quale si presta ai teoremi *evidenti* ed ai problemi *oscuri*, e quale alla scienza *immobile* ed alle opinioni *vacillanti*, e vacillanti sì che *probabili* in un tempo, più che improbabili, compariscano *false* in un altro, quantunque vecchie e radicate: né in temi soltanto *fisici* e *sperimentali*, ma altresì *ideologici, antropologici, cosmologici, morali e giuridici*'. Passaglia, *Sulla dottrina*, 222.
[235] Passaglia, *Sulla dottrina*, 20–23.   [236] Passaglia, *Sulla dottrina*, 59–65.
[237] '*Filosofia Aristotelica* dagli Scolastici esposta e chiosata.' Passaglia, *Sulla dottrina*, 62.

systematiser, rather than as an original author.[238] He excelled in commenting on Aristotle, Passaglia continues, demonstrating expertise in evaluating arguments, resolving complex issues, and selecting appropriate perspectives. However, he suggests that Aquinas could have achieved even greater insights and accuracy if he had had a more comprehensive and detailed understanding of the history of philosophy.[239]

It is important to note, however, that this limitation is also indicative of Aquinas' intellectual greatness. Although he drew upon the philosophical teachings of Aristotle,[240] he was never a mere copyist of the Stagirite. Instead, he freely reworked, commented on and corrected Aristotle's ideas.[241] It is therefore accurate to describe Aquinas as a master in this regard. Through profound and independent investigation – albeit constrained by the resources available to him at the time – he did not uncritically adopt the ideas of Aristotle or other great philosophers of the past. Instead, he reinterpreted them, thereby advancing philosophical inquiry in a way that kept pace with the times.[242]

In his analysis of the encyclical, Passaglia insists on the limitations of Aquinas' philosophical system and the considerable difficulty of absolutising his doctrine. He then proceeds to elucidate the significance of the commendations bestowed upon Aquinas *Aeterni Patris*.[243] In light of Passaglia's considerations, it becomes evident that Aquinas' philosophy is merely an expression of the common philosophical outlook of his time, namely Scholasticism. This in turn can be regarded as a manifestation of the philosophical tradition that has consistently characterised Christian thought. It can therefore be argued that Aquinas' philosophical reflection should be situated within the framework of the so-called 'perennial philosophy'. The term 'perennial philosophy' is used to describe a philosophical tradition that, based on a set of axioms and theorems about God, the world, and human beings, presents its theories in the light of these underlying truths.[244] Accordingly, Passaglia argues that Scholastic philosophy – lauded by the encyclical and understood as a universal philosophical system uniting diverse schools of thought based on a shared vision of God, the world, and human beings – is part of the perennial philosophy.[245] It can thus be concluded that the commendations bestowed upon Scholastic philosophy, and Aquinas' philosophy in *Aeterni Patris* should be understood as an endorsement of perennial philosophy.[246] It follows that this philosophy can be seen as the true philosophical model for the Catholic world.

---

[238] Passaglia, *Sulla dottrina*, 217.   [239] Passaglia, *Sulla dottrina*, 220.
[240] Passaglia, *Sulla dottrina*, 252.   [241] Passaglia, *Sulla dottrina*, 244–245, ft. 5.
[242] Passaglia, *Sulla dottrina*, 256–258.   [243] Passaglia, *Sulla dottrina*, 82.
[244] Passaglia, *Sulla dottrina*, 83.   [245] Passaglia, *Sulla dottrina*, 97–98.
[246] Passaglia, *Sulla dottrina*, 84–95.

3.2.2 The Maximalists and the End of the Freedom of Thought

Against this backdrop, Passaglia's attempt to challenge the tenets of maximalist Thomism becomes clear. His primary focus is not on the philosophy of Aquinas in itself, but rather on the perennial philosophy of which Aquinas's doctrine, with its intrinsic limitations, is part. By proposing a philosophical approach that is open and continuously evolving, and which is grounded within an eclectic idea of philosophy, Passaglia aims to counter the stance of *gli eccessivi* (the Maximalists). This group, which focuses exclusively on Aquinas' thought, regards him as the pinnacle of a self-contained and pyramidal philosophical system, thereby leaving no room for any progress. It follows that, the approach of the maximalists results in a fusion between Christian philosophy and Thomism. Passaglia explicitly questions this idea, arguing: 'Do you really maintain that Aquinas anticipated every philosophical point, leaving us merely to follow in his footsteps? That one must either be a wholehearted Thomist, thereby on the correct path, or, if not a Thomist at all, inevitably stray down oblique and ruinous routes? Such a binary stance strikes me as overly simplistic.'[247]

In light of Plato's claims regarding the impossibility of reaching an absolute and exhaustive knowledge, Passaglia emphasises the duty of scholars to both preserve and advance knowledge.[248] If human beings are always called to advance every field of knowledge, this must also apply to philosophical research, including the study of Aquinas. Commenting on the part of the encyclical that prescribes the restoration of Aquinas' doctrine,[249] Passaglia praises this proposal but simultaneously emphasises that such an endorsement cannot be reduced to merely repeating what Aquinas has already said, presupposing that he has reached perfect and complete knowledge.

It is therefore erroneous to consider Aquinas as the exemplar or archetypal figure of philosophy, despite the assertions of the maximalists.[250] Such an assumption would be tantamount to be anchored to an idealised past conceived as perfect and ideologically re-proposing it into the present, thereby hindering any potential development of understanding.[251]

Passaglia's argument is based on the concept of progress inherent in knowledge.[252] He employs Aquinas' approach to philosophical inquiry as an exemplar, underscoring the significance of safeguarding the autonomy of thought, which is indispensable to any philosophical investigation. Given that

---

[247] 'Secondo voi l'Aquinate, *omne tulit punctum*, a noi non restando che il premerne le tracce? O Tomisti in tutto e per la buona via, o se in parte alcuna non Tomisti, per sentieri obliqui e rovinosi? Mi par troppo.' Passaglia, *Sulla dottrina*, 19–20.
[248] Passaglia, *Sulla dottrina*, 226–227.   [249] *AP*, n. 31.   [250] Passaglia, *Sulla dottrina*, 228.
[251] Passaglia, *Sulla dottrina*, 230–231.   [252] Passaglia, *Sulla dottrina*, 109–112.

philosophical inquiry is continuously subject to change, as an expression of the progress inherent in all human knowledge, it is necessary to adopt an eclectic and original approach to the philosophy of the ancient masters, rather than merely replicating what they have already stated. This approach ensures that the very essence of philosophy, which is founded on development, is maintained. For this reason, Passaglia asserts:

> Let us imitate [the philosophers ...], but not copy them, as the copyist is a parody of the diligent imitator: let us imitate them, not by servilely repeating what they elegantly stated, but by doing what they did, firmly holding fast to immutable dogmas and incontrovertible theorems, but promoting their scientific development .... It would be strange to offer to any philosopher that blind faith which God Himself does not require of his worshippers.[253]

Those who merely reiterate Aquinas' propositions, thereby promoting an ideological Thomism that ultimately leads only to pseudo-Thomism, cannot be considered to be 'pure streams' that flow directly from Aquinas, as they do not genuinely imitate the Angelic Doctor's method of philosophy.[254] These last Aquinas disciples 'though they call themselves Thomists, in fact are not, because they grew up in alien and unhealthy waters'.[255] Conversely, those who can be considered true Thomists are those who are aware of contemporary issues and thus revisit Aquinas' thought and method, studying, deepening and renewing it. These can be considered to be the 'pure streams' of Aquinas, and thus rightfully can be called Thomists. Being aware of the progress and development inherent in philosophical science, they approach Aquinas' doctrine free from any ideological prejudices.[256]

Passaglia, in a polemical manner, identifies Rosmini as an exemplar of an appropriate Thomistic approach, one that is firmly rooted in progress, development, and the freedom of inquiry.[257] Rosmini develops an eclectic philosophical system that adopts Aquinas but does not make him absolute, situating him alongside other significant philosophers. Rosmini, as cited by Passaglia, stated: 'As for the sources from which to draw, I say with full conviction that I do not know any authors who have *doctrines beautiful and fully formed*; however rich

---

[253] 'Imitiamoli [i filosofi ...], ma non li copiamo, ché il copista è la parodia del solerte imitatore: imitiamoli, non già replicando servilmente ciò che essi signorilmente dettarono, bensì facendo quello che essi fecero, tenendo fermi i dogmi immutabili ed i teoremi inconcussi, ma promovendo il loro scientifico svolgimento ...: imperocché sarebbe strano il porgere a qualsivoglia dei filosofi quella *cieca* fede, che Iddio stesso non richiede da' suoi adoratori'. Passaglia, *Sulla dottrina*, 231–232.

[254] Passaglia, *Sulla dottrina*, 270–275.

[255] 'Pur nomandosi *Tomisti*, in effetto nol sono, perché *cresciuti di acque aliene* ed *insalubri*'. Passaglia, *Sulla dottrina*, 275.

[256] Passaglia, *Sulla dottrina*, 263–264.   [257] Passaglia, *Sulla dottrina*, 277–278.

veins of gold are found in Plato, Aristotle, St. Augustine, and St. Thomas Aquinas. Among the moderns, Leibniz and the *two great sophists*, Kant and Hegel, must be read attentively.'[258]

Therefore, if Aquinas, as a philosopher, inquires like other thinkers, and proposes ideas that, although profound, are always subject to development and refutation, then maximalist Thomism, which considers Aquinas as the sole philosophical authority, is an erroneous endeavour that neglects any intellectual progress and the essential freedom of thought in all research fields. Consequently, Passaglia concludes that 'none of us, according to our *Catholic identity*, should be or call ourselves Thomists.'[259]

In conclusion, in light of Passaglia's approach, it can be asserted with Malusa that

> the *Aeterni Patris* represented the completion of the fusion between the horizons of faith and philosophical research. Despite his considerable expertise in the historical and dogmatic aspects of the Immaculate Conception, in vain Passaglia sought to persuade the Neo-Thomists and even members of Leo XIII's entourage that the assertions of dogmatic Thomism and the definitive statements of the encyclical undermined the capacity for both the dynamism of faith and the richness of philosophical inquiry. The former Jesuit highlighted the logical inconsistency of conferring upon Aquinas the same status as the Scriptures and the Councils, thereby stressing that the pontifical authority took a great risk in this operation. As a historian of theology and the great Christian tradition, Passaglia observed the discrepancy between the revealed word and its documents within the Church, as well as the inherent limitations of philosophical research, which is always provisional and, despite its richness, ultimately incomplete.[260]

---

[258] 'Quanto *ai fonti* onde attingere, io le dico *con tutta persuasione* che non v'hanno autori a me noti, che abbiano *le dottrine belle e formate al bisogno*; ma *ricchissime vene* d'oro si trovano in Platone, Aristotile, S. Agostino e S. Tommaso. Fra i moderni è da leggere attentamente Leibnizio, e *i due gran sofisti* Kant ed Hegel'. Passaglia, *Sulla dottrina*, 299.

[259] 'Niun di noi, secondo che *cattolico*, deve essere o chiamarsi *Tomista*'. Passaglia, *Sulla dottrina*, 287.

[260] 'Con la *Aeterni Patris* si compì in modo univoco la fusione tra orizzonte della fede ed orizzonte della ricerca filosofica. Invano proprio il maggiore studioso della verità storica e dogmatica della Immacolata Concezione, il Passaglia, si sforzò di far capire ai neotomisti ed allo stesso *entourage* di Leone XIII che le asserzioni del tomismo dogmatico e le asserzioni perentorie dell'enciclica toglievano spazio tanto al dinamismo della fede quanto alla ricchezza dell'indagine filosofica. L'ex-gesuita mise in luce che era contro la ragione della storia di fare di S. Tommaso filosofo una *auctoritas* pari a quella delle Scritture e dei Concili, e che la autorità pontificia rischiava molto in questo [sic!] operazione. Proprio da storico della teologia e della grande tradizione cristiana nei suoi mille risvolti il Passaglia vedeva la eterogeneità tra la parola rivelata ed i suoi documenti nella Chiesa e la ricerca filosofica, tutta, umana, pur ricca ma sempre provvisoria'. Malusa, *Neotomismo*, vol. 2, 48–49.

3.3 A Comparative Analysis of the Two Perspectives

The most significant insight arising from the comparison between Cornoldi's and Passaglia's approaches is that, despite emerging from the same context, the two authors arrive at diametrically opposed conclusions. This divergence highlights the complexity and multifaceted nature of interpreting *Aeterni Patris* and Thomism at large during this pivotal period. Whereas Cornoldi adopts a more systematic and harmonious reading that seeks to align Thomistic philosophy closely with the papal vision, Passaglia offers a critical stance that questions certain aspects of this interpretation, exposing underlying tensions within the Catholic intellectual milieu. The contrast between their readings not only reflects differing theological and philosophical commitments but also reveals the broader debates concerning the role and scope of Thomism in relation to modernity and the church's socio-political mission.

Both authors, grounded in the classical relationship between faith and reason, emphasise the significance of philosophy for faith. These two realms cannot be separated without falling into a subjectivist and rationalistic philosophy where reason becomes the ultimate authority in itself. Thus, the sphere in which both authors operate is that of Christian philosophy, or, in Passaglia's terms, the 'perennial philosophy'.

Cornoldi reinterprets the relationship between faith and reason in light of the principle of the substantial unity of the soul with the body. In doing so, he eliminates any autonomy of reason, which, in turn, is called to submit to the principle of faith. Against this backdrop, philosophy becomes entirely dependent on the principle of authority, ultimately represented by faith itself. Consequently, faith, posited as the definitive criterion of philosophy, serves to ascertain the veracity of philosophical reasoning. The implicit consequence of this reasoning leads to the conclusion that the church is the ultimate authority in the philosophical field, given its role in regulating and determining matters of faith. It follows that philosophy must be subject to the ecclesiastical magisterium. In light of these premises, the Venetian Jesuit deems the approach of the church Fathers and Scholastics to be an exemplar of such a philosophical method, with Aquinas representing the pinnacle of such a model. Thomism is thus conceived as the only perfect and complete philosophy that must be adopted and imitated; in other words, it becomes the authoritative and certain model of Christian philosophy.[261] Consequently, the advancement of philosophical thought, namely a genuine philosophical progress, consists in reviving Aquinas' philosophy. Furthermore, the attainment of true freedom lies in

---

[261] Malusa, *Neotomismo*, vol. 2, 25–26.

offering docile obedience to the teachings of the church, which has sanctioned Thomism as the sole Christian philosophy.

Conversely, Passaglia's philosophical outlook is informed by a different understanding of the relationship between faith and reason, which differs from the perspective espoused by Cornoldi. While Cornoldi explicitly employs the principle of substantial unity to elucidate the interconnection between *fides* and *ratio*, Passaglia, in contrast, grounds his reasoning in the Chalcedonian principle pertaining to the relationship between Christ's two natures. The former Jesuit argues that although faith and reason are unified, they should not be confused or mixed.[262] It is therefore imperative that all aspects of faith are accepted as true. However, it is equally crucial that all matters falling within the domain of reason be freely studied and investigated through the use of all appropriate methods of rational inquiry. If this principle applies to theology – which, for Passaglia, is considered the science of faith, distinct from faith itself, thus requiring a scientific and rational approach – [263] it applies even more so to philosophy, which investigates natural truths that are entirely dependent on reason.

Therefore, in accordance with the principles of free rational inquiry, Passaglia advocates for a comprehensive and nuanced understanding of philosophical knowledge. His approach to philosophy is not constrained by the limitations of a specific intellectual tradition, such as Thomism, but rather, it is an open and evolving perspective. Therefore, like other philosophical systems, Thomism is conceived as a moment within the entire philosophical development and cannot be considered the model for all Christian philosophy. According to Passaglia, the most suitable philosophical model for Christian philosophy is the 'perennial philosophy', which is based on a harmonious relationship between faith and reason. As the model in question cannot be fully encompassed, given the ongoing evolution of knowledge, it is essential to pursue further investigation through the utilisation of the full range of scientific instruments that have been developed over time for philosophical inquiry. For Passaglia, the continuous advancement of 'perennial philosophy' is predicated on the liberty of thought and the utilisation of an eclectic methodology.

In conclusion, it may be asserted that the fundamental distinction between the two approaches lies precisely in the principle adopted as their point of departure. If, grounded in the principle of substantial unity, faith is conceived as the

---

[262] The application of the Chalcedonian Christological doctrine, which seeks to achieve a harmonisation of the opposites, is a defining feature of Passaglia's thought. This doctrine is evident in his approach to ecclesiology, anthropology and also in his conceptualisation of the relationship between the church and the State: Passaglia, *De ecclesia*. Passaglia, *Conferenze*.

[263] Passaglia, *Sulla dottrina*, 131.

form of reason, it follows that reason is thereby deprived of its own subsistence and autonomy. This leads to a system founded on authority, in which neither intellectual autonomy nor genuine progress in research is feasible. Conversely, in accordance with the Chalcedonian principle, if faith and reason are understood as two distinct entities that, despite their union, preserve their respective identities and autonomy, then the autonomy of reason is affirmed, thereby establishing a philosophical system grounded in the freedom of inquiry and the progressive development of knowledge.

Applying the Chalcedonian analogy to the relationship between faith and reason underscores the possibility of a harmonious yet distinct coexistence, allowing each domain to flourish within its own parameters. Such a framework not only safeguards the integrity of philosophical inquiry but also facilitates constructive dialogue between theology and philosophy. It thus provides a compelling model for Catholic thought, one that embraces both fidelity to revealed truth and openness to intellectual development.

Conclusion: From Ideological Thomism to Historical Thomism

This study on the revival of Thomism initiated by Leo XIII's *Aeterni Patris* has illuminated the central role of this encyclical within Catholic intellectual history, as well as the ideological impetus behind the renewed emphasis on Thomistic philosophy. Thomism re-emerged as a leading current within the broader movement of the intransigent Catholicism, which sought to re-establish Aquinas' thought as a unified philosophical system capable of articulating a coherent Christian worldview in opposition to the rationalist currents of modernity.

A historical analysis of this revival reveals that ideological motivations were embedded in Thomism from its inception. Initially, the Thomistic movement arose in the early nineteenth century as a manifestation of Italian Catholic counter-revolutionary thought, synthesising elements of French traditionalism with Aquinas' philosophy in resistance to the rationalist and liberal ideals propagated by the French Revolution. While this early Thomism remained marginal within a Catholic intellectual milieu still marked by pluralism, it gained traction through the efforts of the Jesuits of *La Civiltà Cattolica*, whose promotion of a maximalist Thomism between the 1850s and 1870s laid the groundwork for its later institutional ascendancy. It was within this context that *Aeterni Patris* became the catalyst for consolidating Thomism as the normative framework of Catholic philosophy.

Aeterni Patris must be situated within the broader reformist agenda of Leo XIII, already prefigured in his inaugural encyclical *Inscrutabili Dei consilio*, wherein the philosophical problem of the relationship between faith and reason is shown to be inextricably linked to the exigencies of the social order. Within this perspective, philosophy is not conceived as a merely speculative enterprise, but as an essential instrument for the preservation and restoration of human and societal values threatened by the corrosive dynamics of modern rationalism. In this framework, the philosophical question reveals itself as inseparable from the social question, the two being mutually implicated in the project of cultural and moral regeneration. Hence, Leo XIII's decision to dedicate an entire encyclical to a philosophical theme – arguably beyond the immediate purview of the magisterium – thus attests to the gravity with which he perceived the crisis afflicting both the intellectual and civil spheres.

The principal aim of *Aeterni Patris* was the restoration of a philosophical tradition founded upon the indissoluble harmony between faith and reason. Within this intellectual paradigm, authentic philosophy is understood as a disciplined inquiry into truth conducted under the light of faith. Far from diminishing reason, faith is conceived as its elevation and perfection: it renders accessible those supernatural truths that surpass the capacities of unaided human reason, while simultaneously conferring greater depth and certitude to the apprehension of natural truths. Reason, for its part, is not regarded as an independent or antagonistic faculty vis-à-vis faith, but rather as its indispensable instrument. In this sense, the classical model of philosophy as the handmaid of theology (*philosophia ancilla theologiae*) is emphatically reaffirmed. The encyclical's retrieval of this model is to be read as a deliberate and programmatic response to the modern fracture between the domains of faith and rational inquiry.

Within this framework, the encyclical advocates a return to Aquinas' doctrine, which is regarded as the pinnacle and culmination of Christian philosophical thought. However, in identifying Thomism as the privileged expression of Christian philosophy, *Aeterni Patris* implicitly risks a reduction of the Christian intellectual tradition to a single doctrinal system. If Thomism is portrayed as both the apex and exclusive vehicle of Christian thought, its revival becomes a socio-political project aimed at reconstructing a Christian order. Here, the ideological dimension becomes evident: Aquinas is invoked not primarily as a subject of historical inquiry, but as a normative authority enlisted to combat the perceived errors of modernity. Once again, the ideological and ahistorical dimension underlying such an operation becomes evident.

Even initiatives such as the establishment of the *Commissio Leonina* – ostensibly conceived to produce a critical and scholarly edition of Aquinas' corpus – remained, in large measure, circumscribed by the ideological framework inaugurated by the encyclical. Rather than promoting a genuinely historical and philologically grounded engagement with Aquinas' thought, such undertakings often served to reinforce a utilitarian appropriation of his philosophy, wherein Aquinas functioned as the *auctoritas* to refute the internal incoherence of rationalist positions and to substantiate the truth claims of the Christian intellectual tradition. In this context, his work ceased to be the object of disinterested inquiry and became instead an instrument employed in the service of an apologetic and polemical agenda.

In light of these considerations, it becomes apparent that a form of circular reinforcement exists between the ahistorical and ideological presuppositions underlying Leo XIII's *Aeterni Patris* and the maximalist interpretations that emerged in its wake. This dynamic is particularly evident in the commentary of Cornoldi, which can be considered as the authoritative interpretation of the encyclical. Cornoldi's maximalist reading, gave rise to a form of Thomism that has been defined as 'essential Thomism'. This interpretive model reduces the complexity of Aquinas' thought to a series of foundational principles construed as the definitive expression of his philosophical doctrine. The basic premise of this approach is that a grasp of these essential tenets is equivalent to an exhaustive understanding of Aquinas' system as a whole.

Such a radical simplification – though not explicitly endorsed by the encyclical – is the result of a retrospective, ideologically motivated appropriation of selected aspects of Aquinas' corpus. At its core lies the attempt to delimit the interpretive field by means of a fixed hermeneutical framework, within which Aquinas' philosophy is reconfigured as a systematic and unified body of thought. This hermeneutical constraint, far from fostering a critical engagement with the Thomistic tradition, aims rather at securing doctrinal uniformity and precluding alternative or pluralistic readings.

Once again, the absence of historical consciousness inherent in this interpretive approach becomes manifest. When Aquinas' philosophy is reduced to a fixed set of foundational principles – deemed essential and normative – the focus inevitably shifts from critical engagement with the internal complexity and historical development of his thought to a mere reiteration and defence of these extracted propositions. Paradoxically, the very school of maximalist Thomism that aspires to present Aquinas as the unsurpassable model of Christian philosophy is, in fact, the product of a reductive and uncritical appropriation of his intellectual legacy. In summary, the concept of 'essential Thomism' represents an attempt to make Aquinas' thought absolute by defining certain philosophical principles as essential, with the objective of eliminating pluralism and establishing a simple and unified system of thought capable of opposing modern society.

Although the maximalist current would come to exert considerable influence within Catholic intellectual circles, it did not emerge as the sole or uncontested interpretive framework. In this regard, the commentary of Passaglia – arguably formulated as a direct rejoinder to Cornoldi's reading – presents a markedly different approach to *Aeterni Patris* and to the role of Thomism more broadly. Employing a historical-critical method rooted in a positivist hermeneutic, Passaglia offers a scientifically rigorous exegesis of the encyclical, foregrounding the broader question of Christian philosophy as a living tradition rather than a closed system.

Through this lens, Aquinas is not conceived as the exclusive or definitive culmination of Christian philosophical reflection, but rather as one eminent representative within a more extensive and pluralistic continuum. Passaglia's perspective thus relativises the centrality of Thomism, situating it within the broader historical unfolding of Christian thought. By recovering the diachronic dimension of the tradition, his interpretation effectively neutralises the latent tendencies toward doctrinal maximalism already implicit in the encyclical, and simultaneously undermines those readings that seek to render Aquinas' philosophy absolute and normative in all contexts.

In so doing, Passaglia opens the way toward a more historically conscious and intellectually open framework for engaging with the Thomistic legacy – one that resists ideological closure and affirms the legitimacy of diverse philosophical articulations within the Christian tradition.

Nevertheless, it was not until the early twentieth century that Thomistic studies experienced a significant advancement, thereby emancipating themselves from their original ideological frameworks. The most consequential contribution to this development is attributable to Étienne Gilson and his historical investigations into Scholasticism and medieval philosophy. Paradoxically, the French scholar rehabilitated Thomism precisely on the basis of the very accusation that had contributed to its marginalisation throughout the nineteenth century – namely, that Thomism was primarily theological rather than philosophical in nature.

Gilson's historical methodology, shaped by his secular academic formation, led him to the conclusion that neither Thomism nor Scholasticism as a whole could be properly regarded as autonomous philosophical systems. This conclusion rested on the observation that the context in which these traditions emerged, the problems they addressed, and the manner in which they addressed them were fundamentally theological. Accordingly, a proper engagement with Aquinas's thought requires an awareness of the ideological presuppositions that sought to interpret his philosophy as a unified and self-contained system, abstracted from its historical context.

Aquinas's thought, therefore, ought not to be reduced to a flawless philosophical doctrine to be employed as an absolute model of Christian thought, in contrast to modern philosophical systems. Nor should it be treated as a kind of manual for resolving the moral or intellectual challenges of contemporary society.

Moreover, according to Gilson, it is equally untenable to reduce the entire tradition of Christian thought to Thomism, for such an approach fails to grasp the proper meaning of the concept of Christian philosophy. It is a mistake to equate Christian philosophy either with Scholasticism or with Thomism. Likewise, it is historically inaccurate to present Scholasticism as the dominant or exclusive philosophical paradigm of the Middle Ages. To conflate these categories is a conceptual fallacy. What unites the great medieval thinkers is not Scholasticism per se, but rather a mode of inquiry grounded in faith and revelation – what Gilson identifies as Christian philosophy – which, in turn, is articulated through a variety of philosophical frameworks, among which Scholasticism is but one.

As the French philosopher states:

> By the time Christian thought had reached a more advanced stage, it was no longer conceivable to suppose that a single philosophy was commonly taught by Saint Anselm, Saint Thomas Aquinas, Saint Bonaventure, John Duns Scotus, and William of Ockham. It had become evident that, although these masters employed distinct philosophical frameworks, they all affirmed the same truth of Christian revelation received through faith. They thus arrived at the same religious truth by means of diverse philosophical paths. This fundamental agreement imparted a certain unity to their doctrines – not merely in the conclusions they reached, but also in the spirit that animated their intellectual pursuits. If one seeks the cause of this shared orientation, the only adequate explanation lies in the common Christian character of their inquiry.[264]

In light of these considerations, it becomes evident that the thought of Aquinas – like that of other eminent Scholastic masters – constitutes one component within the broader Christian tradition, a tradition that undertakes

---

[264] 'L'éetude de la pensée chrétienne était déjà trop avancée pour qu'on pût encore imaginer une philosophie, une et la même, qu'auraient enseignée en commun saint Anselme, saint Thomas d'Aquin, saint Bonaventure, Jean Duns Scot et Guillaume Ockham. Il était d'autre part évident que bien qu'ils missent en œuvre des philosophies différentes, ces maîtres tenaient pour accordéela vérité de la révélation chrétienne reçue par la foi. Ils rejoignaient donc la même vérité religieuse par des voies philosophiques diverses, et cet accord fondamental contribuait à conférer une sorte d'unité à l'ensemble de ces doctrines, non seulement dans la lettre des conclusions, mais dans l'esprite de la recherche. Si l'on s'interroge sur la cause de cet accord, la seule concevable est leur caractère chrétien'. Gilson, *Le philosophe*, 159–160.

rational inquiry in the light of Revelation. Consequently, Thomism cannot be regarded as absolute or exhaustive in itself.

Although Gilson arrived at these conclusions through the course of his historical research beginning in the early twentieth century, it is noteworthy that he found confirmation for his position in *Aeterni Patris*.[265] When he first became acquainted with the encyclical in the 1930s, it immediately became clear to him that the central issue addressed by the papal document was not merely the revival of Thomism, but rather the broader theme of Christian philosophy. Gilson thus contends that to engage in philosophical inquiry *ad mentem Sancti Thomae* (in accordance with the thought of St. Thomas Aquinas), as prescribed by the encyclical, does not entail the absolutisation of Aquinas's thought. On the contrary, it involves adopting a philosophical posture analogous to that of Aquinas himself – namely, a mode of reason that operates in the light of faith.[266] Accordingly, Gilson's interpretation maintains that the significance of the encyclical lies not in any implausible attempt to 'dogmatise' Thomism, but rather in the reaffirmation of the concept of Christian philosophy and in the presentation of Aquinas as one of the central figures in the history of Christian thought.

While Gilson's interpretation bears a resemblance to that of Passaglia – likely due to their shared historical-critical methodology – it is significant that, unlike Passaglia, Gilson did not discern the political and social dimensions underlying Leo XIII's encyclical, nor did he perceive the risk of Thomistic maximalism that *Aeterni Patris* arguably entails.

In conclusion, it may be affirmed that, according to Gilson, the fundamental flaw in the modern recovery of Thomism does not lie in the fact that Aquinas's doctrine is essentially theological rather than properly philosophical, but rather in the ahistorical and uncritical manner in which Thomism has often been appropriated. This approach seeks to convert Aquinas's thought into a comprehensive philosophical system, employed ideologically to counter the perceived errors of modernity. The incompatibility between Gilson's historical methodology and this ideological appropriation is illustrated by the numerous criticisms he received from within Catholic circles, particularly from Thomists who continued to uphold a maximalist interpretation of Thomism.

Although Gilson's perspective represents a decisive turning point in Thomistic studies and a significant advance in the contemporary study of medieval philosophy, it must be acknowledged that within Catholicism – especially in ecclesiastical institutions – the ahistorical and ideologically driven

---

[265] Gilson, *Le philosophe*, 157–178.   [266] Gilson, *Le philosophe*, 165–166.

model of Thomism has endured, and in certain respects continues to exert influence even today.[267] It is therefore imperative to remain critically attentive to the historical developments that have contributed to making Aquinas one of the most significant, albeit contested, figures in the landscape of modern Catholic thought – an awareness that this study has sought to cultivate.

---

[267] Malusa, *Neotomismo*, vol. 1, XVII.

Bibliography

Acta Sanctae Sedis in compendium oportune redacta et illustrata, vol. 12, Romae 1879: 97–115.

Bianchini, Paolo. 'La *Ratio Studiorum* alla prova della modernità: Le revisioni del piano di studi e della pedagogia della Compagnia di Gesù tra XVIII e XIX secolo'. *Rivista di Storia del Cristianesimo* 11 (2014): 325–340.

Buzzetti, Vincenzo. *Institutiones sanae philosophiae iuxta Divi Thomae atque Aristotelis inconcussa dogmata*. 2 vol. Edited by A. Masnovo. Merlini, 1940–1941.

Calvetti, Giuseppe. 'Del progresso filosofico possibile nel tempo presente'. *La Civiltà Cattolica* serie II, 3 (1853): 265–287.

Carola, Joseph. *Engaging the Church Fathers in Nineteenth-Century Catholicism: The Patristic Legacy of the* Scuola Romana. Emmaus Academic, 2023.

Colapietra, Raffaele. *La chiesa tra Lamennais e Metternich: Il pontificato di Leone XII*. Morcelliana, 1963.

Congar, Yves. *A History of Theology*. Translated and edited by H. Guthrie. Doubleday, 1968.

Cornoldi, Giovanni M. 'La regola filosofica di sua Santità Leone P.P. XIII proposta nell'enciclica *Aeterni Patris*'. *La Civiltà Cattolica* serie X, 11 (1879): 657–672; 12 (1879): 165–183; 272–290; 425–443; 529–547 = *La riforma della filosofia promossa dall'enciclica Aeterni Patris di S.S. Leone XIII*. Mareggiani, 1880.

Curci, Carlo M. 'Il giornalismo moderno e il nostro programma'. *La Civiltà Cattolica* serie I, 1 (1850): 5–24.

Curci, Carlo M. 'Le nostre speranze'. *La Civiltà Cattolica* serie I, 5 (1851): 5–16.

Curci, Carlo M. 'Il fatto e il da farsi'. *La Civiltà Cattolica* serie I, 11 (1852): 5–23; 129–142.

De Rosa, Gabriele. 'Introduzione'. In *Civiltà Cattolica 1850–1945: Antologia*. Vol. 1. Edited by G. De Rosa. Landi Editore, 1971: 9–101.

Del Chiaro, Giuseppe, ed. *Indice generale della Civiltà Cattolica (aprile 1850 dicembre 1903)*. Tipi della Civiltà Cattolica, 1904.

Dezza, Paolo. *Alle origini del neotomismo*. Bocca, 1940.

Filograssi, Giuseppe. 'Teologia e filosofia nel Collegio Romano dal 1824 ad oggi'. *Gregorianum* 35 (1954): 512–540.

Fontana, Sandro. *La controrivoluzione cattolica in Italia (1820–1830)*. Morcelliana, 1968.

Fontana, Sandro. 'Vincenzo Buzzetti'. In *Dizionario biografico degli Italiani*: bit.ly/4faPBet.
Gilson, Étienne. *Le Thomisme. Introduction au système de S. Thomas d'Aquin*. Vix, 1919.
Gilson, Étienne. *La philosphie au Moyen âge*. Payot, 1922.
Gilson, Étienne. *Le philosophe et la théologie*. Vrin, 2005.
Giovagnoli, Agostino. *Dalla teologia alla politica: L'itinerario di Carlo Passaglia negli anni di Pio IX e Cavour*. Morcelliana, 1984.
Guerci, Luciano. *Uno spettacolo non mai più veduto nel mondo. La rivoluzione francese come unicità e rovesciamento negli scrittori controrivoluzionari italiani (1789–1799)*. UTET, 2008.
Hegel, Georg W. F. *Lectures on the History of Philosophy*. Vol. 3. Translated by E. Haldane and F. Simon. Trübner, 1896.
Kasper, Walter. *Die Lehre von der Tradition in der Römischen Schule*. Herder, 2011.
Kerkvoorde, Augustine. 'La théologie du "corps mystique" au dix-neuvieme siècle'. *Nouvelle Revue Théologique* 67 (1945): 1025–1038.
Lamberts, Emiel. 'Religious, Political and Social Settings of the Revival of Thomism, 1870–1960'. In *Ne-Thomism in Action: Law and Society Reshaped by Neo-Scholastic Philosophy, 1880–1960*. Edited by W. Decock, B. Raymaekers and P. Heyrman. Leuven University Press, 2021: 29–39.
Leo XII. Breve pontificio *Cum multa in Urbe*. 16 May 1824. bit.ly/4f9uUjd.
Leo XIII. Encyclical Letter *Inscrutabili Dei consilio*. 21 April 1878. bit.ly/3ZpBnAw.
Leo XIII. Encyclical Letter *Aeterni Patris. De philosophia christiana ad mentem Sancti Thomae Aquinatis in scholis catholicis instauranda*. 4 August 1879. bit.ly/41nZ4f2.
Leo XIII. Epistola *Iampridem considerando*. 15 October 1879. bit.ly/3D6cYbK.
Leo XIII. Motu Proprio *Placere nobis*. 18 January 1880. bit.ly/41snZOH.
Leo XIII. *Acta*. Vol. 1. Typographia Vaticana, 1881.
Leo XIII. Encyclical Letter *Immortale Dei*. 1 November 1885. bit.ly/3OLOo2v.
Leo XIII. *Allocutiones, epistolae, constitutiones aliaque acta praecipua*. Vol. 1 (1878–1882). Desclée, 1887.
Levering Matthew, Pidel Aaron and Anderson Justin M., eds. *The Roman School*. Brill 2024.
Liberatore, Matteo. 'L'enciclica del S. Padre Leone XIII'. *La Civiltà Cattolica* serie X, 6 (1878): 513–523; 641–652.

Malusa, Luciano. *Neotomismo e intransigentismo cattolico*. 2 Vols. Istituto di Propaganda Libraria, 1986–1989.

Marschler, Thomas. 'Nineteenth-Century Catholic Reception of Aquinas'. In *The Oxford Handbook of the Reception of Aquinas*. Edited by M. Levering and M. Plested. Oxford University Press, 2021, 148–165.

Martina, Giacomo. 'Il Collegio Romano: 1824–1873'. *Roma moderna e contemporanea* 3 (1995): 667–691.

Masnovo, Amato. *Il neo-tomismo in Italia: Origini e prime vicende*. Vita e Pensiero, 1923.

Masnovo, Amato. 'Il discorso commemorativo'. In *Alle origini del neotomismo*. Edited by P. Dezza. Bocca, 1940: 148–165.

Mattiussi, Guido. *Le XXIV tesi della filosofia di San Tommaso d'Aquino approvate dalla S. Congregazione degli studi*. Befani, 1917.

Pachtler, Georg Michael, and Bernard Duhr, eds. *Ratio studiorum et institutiones scholasticae Societatis Iesu per Germaniam olim vigentes collectae concinnatae*. Hofmann, 1887.

Passaglia, Carlo. *De ecclesia Christi*. 2 vols. Manz, 1853–1856.

Passaglia, Carlo. *De immaculato Deiparae semper Virginis Conceptu*. Pars 3. Propaganda Fide, 1855.

Passaglia, Carlo. *Conferenze di Diritto Pubblico*. Il mediatore, 1864.

Passaglia, Carlo. *Sulla dottrina di San Tommaso secondo l'enciclica di Leone XIII*. Paravia, 1880.

Passaglia, Carlo, and Clemens Schrader, eds. 'Editorum Praefatio'. In *Dyonisii Petavii aurelianensis e S.I. opus de theologicis dogmatibus expolitum et auctum collatis studiis Car. Passaglia et Clem. Schrader*, Propaganda Fide, 1857: 59–76.

Perini, Giuseppe. 'Dall' "Aeterni Patris" al Concilio Vaticano II: le direttive del magistero sulla dottrina di san Tommaso'. *Scripta Theologica* 11 (1979): 619–658.

Perrone, Giovanni. *Praelectiones Theologicae*. Vol. 2, pars 2. Typis Collegii Urbani, 1842.

Pius IX. Breve pontificio *Gravissimum supremi*. 12 February 1866. *La Civiltà Cattolica* serie VI, 6 (1866): 7–15.

Piolanti, Antonio. *Il tomismo come filosofia cristiana nel pensiero di Leone XIII*. Libreria Editrice Vaticana, 1983.

Pirri, Pietro. 'Il p. Taparelli d'Azeglio e il rinnovamento della scolastica al Collegio Romano 1825–1829'. In *L'università Gregoriana del Collegio Romano nel primo secolo dalla restituzione*. Cuggiani, 1924: 59–76.

Pirri, Pietro. 'Intorno alle origini del rinnovamento tomista in Italia. Il P. Taparelli e il P. Sordi'. *La Civiltà Cattolica* 79 (1928): 215–229; 396–411.

Rafferty, Oliver P. 'The Thomistic Revival and the Relationship between the Jesuits and the Papacy, 1878–1914'. *Theological Studies* 75 (2014): 746–773.

Rossi, Giovanni Felice. 'La neoscolastica italiana dalle sue prime manifestazioni all'enciclica "Aeterni Patris"'. *Rivista di Filosofia Neo-scolastica* 82 (1990): 365–411.

Rossi, Valfredo Maria. 'Carlo Passaglia and Pius IX: An ecclesiological conflict'. *The Journal of Ecclesiastical History* 71 (2020): 579–595.

Rossi, Valfredo Maria. 'Giovanni Fortunato Zamboni (1756–1850) and the Unpublished Manuscript of the *Riflessioni*. A Secret Plan to Re-establish the *Societas Christiana*'. *Revue d'histoire ecclésiastique* 118 (2023): 145–167.

Sandoni, Luca, ed. *Il Sillabo di Pio IX*. Clueb & Casa editrice Università La Sapienza, 2012.

Schauf, Heribert. 'Carl Passaglia und Clemens Schrader. Beitrag zur Theologiegeschichte des neunzehnten Jahrhunderts'. PhD diss., Pontifical Gregorian University, 1938.

Schrader, Clemens. *De hominum societate generatim*: Commentarius. In *Theses theologicae. Series septima*. Mayer, 1869.

Shea, C. Michael. '*Ressourcement* in the Age of Migne: The Jesuit Theologians of the *Collegio Romano* and the Shape of Modern Catholic Thought'. *Nova et Vetera* (English Edition) 15 (2017): 579–613.

Shea, C. Michael. *Newman's Early Roman Catholic Legacy*. Oxford University Press, 2017.

Silvestrelli, Antonio. 'Le fonti immediate dell'enciclica "Aeterni Patris" e la sua struttura'. In *L'enciclica Aeterni Patris, Significato e preparazione. Atti dell'VIII Congresso Tomistico Internazionale*. Vol. 2. Libreria Editrice Vaticana, 1981: 138–150.

Sulas, Cinzia. 'La riforma della *Ratio studiorum* di fronte al paradigma scientifio moderno. La prospettiva di Luigi Taparelli SJ, rettore al Collegio Romano (1824–182)'. *Archivum historicum Societatis Iesu* 86 (2017): 301–336.

Taparelli d'Azeglio, Luigi. 'Di due filosofie'. *La Civiltà Cattolica* serie II, 1 (1853): 369–380; 481–506; 626–647.

Taparelli d'Azeglio, Luigi. 'Terza serie della Civiltà Cattolica'. *La Civiltà Cattolica* serie II, 12 (1855): 609–629.

Traniello, Francesco. *Cattolicesimo conciliatorista: Religione e cultura nella tradizione rosminiana lombardo-piemontese (1825–1870)*. Morzati, 1970.

Tutino, Stefania. *Empire of Souls: Robert Bellarmine and the Christian Commonwealth*. Oxford University Press, 2010.

Ventura, Gioacchino. *De methodo philosophandi: Pars prima de philosophia et methodo philosophandi in genere*. Perego-Salvioni, 1828.

Ventura, Gioacchino. *Osservazioni sulle opinioni filosofiche dei Signori De Bonald, De Maistre, De La Mennais e Lurentie all'occaione di un articolo del giornale francese* Il Corrispondente *indirizzate al signore editore dello stesso giornale dal P.D. Gioacchino Ventura teatino*. Perego-Salvioni, 1829.

Vian, Giovanni. 'Luigi Taparelli d'Azeglio'. In *Enciclopedia Italiana. Il contributo italiano alla storia del pensiero – storia e politica*, 2013. bit.ly/4gqZ1U2.

Cambridge Elements

History of Philosophy and Theology in the West

Alexander J. B. Hampton
University of Toronto
Alexander J. B. Hampton is a professor at the University of Toronto, specialising in metaphysics, poetics, and nature. His publications include *Romanticism and the Re-Invention of Modern Religion* (Cambridge 2019), *Christian Platonism: A History* (ed.) (Cambridge, 2021), and the *Cambridge Companion to Christianity and the Environment* (ed.) (Cambridge, 2022).

Editorial Board
Shaun Blanchard, *University of Notre Dame, Australia*
Jennifer Newsome Martin, *University of Notre Dame, USA*
Sean McGrath, *Memorial University*
Willemien Otten, *University of Chicago*
Catherine Pickstock, *University of Cambridge*
Jacob H. Sherman, *California Institute of Integral Studies*
Charles Taliaferro, *St. Olaf College*

About the Series
In the history of philosophy and theology, many figures and topics are considered in isolation from each other. This series aims to complicate this binary opposition, while covering the history of this complex conversation from antiquity to the present. It reconceptualizes traditional elements of the field, generating new and productive areas of historical enquiry, and advancing creative proposals based upon the recovery of these resources.

Cambridge Elements⁼

History of Philosophy and Theology in the West

Elements in the Series

The Metaphysics of Divine Participation
Alexander J. B. Hampton

C. S. Lewis on the Soul, God, and Christianity
Stewart Goetz

Popper, Philosophy and Faith
Anthony O'Hear

Leo XIII and the Rise of Neo-Thomism
Valfredo Maria Rossi

A full series listing is available at: www.cambridge.org/EHPT

Printed by Libri Plureos GmbH in Hamburg, Germany